Beyond Bias

Unleashing the Potential of Women in Law

Second Edition

EDITED BY FRANCESCA RAMADAN

Commissioning editor
Francesca Ramadan

Managing director
Sian O'Neill

Beyond Bias: Unleashing the Potential of Women in Law, Second Edition
is published by

Globe Law and Business Ltd
3 Mylor Close
Horsell
Woking
Surrey GU21 4DD
United Kingdom
Tel: +44 20 3745 4770
www.globelawandbusiness.com

Beyond Bias: Unleashing the Potential of Women in Law, Second Edition

ISBN 978-1-83723-137-9
EPUB ISBN 978-1-83723-138-6
Adobe PDF ISBN 978-1-83723-139-3

Contents

Executive summary

Published in 2017, the first edition of *Beyond Bias: Unleashing the Potential of Women in Law* considered just how much firms were losing by their failure to retain and promote women lawyers; the reasons why their efforts to better achieve these objectives had seen so little return; and the practical steps firms could take to move the needle in regard to the absence of women in positions of power. Nearly ten years on, both much and little has changed: according to recent data from the Solicitors Regulation Authority, which will be further explored within the following pages, women now outnumber men within the UK's legal profession, but a seniority gap persists.[1] These trends are reflected on a global scale: from survey data collected across 12 countries by the International Bar Association, it has been demonstrated that, on average, women make up 47 percent of all lawyers, but only 38 percent are in senior positions, with the largest gaps between the number of female lawyers overall and the number of female lawyers in positions of responsibility occurring in Chile, England and Wales, and Spain.[2]

However, the problems in achieving parity within the legal profession extend far beyond the number of women in its upper echelons. Despite decades of effort, the profession remains one of the least diverse, with systemic barriers affecting who enters, advances, and succeeds. Bias – whether conscious or unconscious – perpetuates inequality, impacting hiring, promotions, pay, and leadership opportunities. The traditional pipeline to success in legal practice favors those with economic privilege, established networks, and cultural capital, leaving others at a disadvantage. The statistics are shocking: for instance, in the UK, only 19 percent of lawyers within law firms are from a non-White ethnic background.[3] Similarly, only 6 percent are disabled; a mere 4.4 percent identify as LGBTQ+; and the number of lawyers from deprived socioeconomic backgrounds has actually reduced from 21 percent in 2015 to 18 percent in 2023.[4]

To overcome this, our understanding of the work needed to achieve gender parity in the legal profession must expand to encompass the deeper and more nuanced insights an intersectional approach can offer. Application of an intersectional perspective enables us to better understand and navigate the barriers that hinder different (and often historically overlooked) groups of women lawyers, rendering efforts to achieve gender equality more targeted, effective, and inclusive, thereby empowering all women – not just the select few. An old adage frames this as such: "A rising tide lifts all boats." While previous discussions on gender discrimination have largely focused on the efforts of the individual to overcome the obstacles to women's success in law, the issue is far larger – from the exclusion of varied pathways to partnership to the hidden costs of ageism and the burden of respectability politics. This second edition of *Beyond Bias: Unleashing the Potential of Women in Law* provides a comprehensive analysis of the barriers to true equity for women in law, and what can be done to overcome these at the systemic level. At a time when diversity, equity, and inclusion (DEI) initiatives are under fire, this book makes the business case for gender equity, showing how inclusive teams drive better decision-making, innovation, and profitability. Written by women lawyers who have achieved success, despite the odds, and leading experts who have helped law firms and corporations implement meaningful change, this book is more than just an exploration of the problem – it is a roadmap for transforming the legal profession into one that truly reflects the diversity of the world it serves, offering a holistic, nuanced examination of women's journeys, achievements, and challenges in law and the ways in which firms and practitioners can implement meaningful change.

We begin by asking a critical question: what is intersectionality, and why does it matter? Chapter 1, authored by Brie Stevens-Hoare KC, barrister at Gatehouse Chambers, examines the academic foundation of intersectionality; the story the statistics can tell us; and real-world examples of the challenges faced by all types of women in the legal profession. Consideration of some of the fundamental differences between characteristics (for instance, the visible and the invisible) enriches our understanding of what we can learn from individuals' lived experiences, both in wider society and in the legal profession. Brie then explores the ways in which an intersectional approach – in its capacity to highlight both shared and diverse experiences – can enhance our awareness of the barriers to women's success in law, and what it can teach us about ways to address those barriers. The lessons we can learn from the experiences of those who are LGBTQIA+, neurodiverse, disabled, or from a minority ethnic or socioeconomically disadvantaged background are examined in greater depth. Finally, this chapter considers the risks of an intersectional perspective, balanced by an exploration of the practical tools and approaches offered by intersectionality to tackle not just bias, but structural or institutional barriers.

Our examination of systemic bias and barriers to women's success in law continues in Chapter 2. Historically, leadership in the legal profession has been framed through a narrow, masculine-coded lens, prioritizing traits such as assertiveness, dominance, and detachment. For decades, women in law were advised to adopt these behaviors to succeed, often at the cost of authenticity, wellbeing, and connection. Drawing on both lived experience and emerging leadership research, Rachel Spink, founder of Female Lawyers' Club, challenges these outdated norms and asks: what if the very qualities traditionally seen as "feminine" – such as empathy, collaboration, emotional intelligence, and inclusivity – are not signs of weakness, but are instead the foundations of great leadership? This chapter will examine the ways in which rigid leadership archetypes have contributed to the underrepresentation of women at the top and proposes a more expansive model that allows diverse leadership styles to thrive. To guide practitioners and firms in championing this new conception of leadership, Rachel includes practical examples of the myriad ways in which embracing these traits benefits teams, enhances performance, and supports sustainable careers. Rachel offers a new vision of legal leadership – one that works not only *for* women, but *because* of them.

Women's success in law is not only impacted by historically embedded bias and barriers; it is also increasingly shaped by the digital tools that are quickly becoming essential to modern legal practice. Artificial intelligence (AI) is one such influencing factor. In Chapter 3, Priya Lele, chair and cofounder of She Breaks the Law, and Shilpa Bhandarkar, legal innovation and AI consultant, explore the risks and opportunities that AI – and, in particular, the new wave of generative AI – presents for women, and its potential impact on the gender gap in law. Priya and Shilpa begin with an overview of the gender disparities in AI development, design, and deployment, and examine how these broader trends are reflected in the legal sector. Critically, Priya and Shilpa explore the reasons *why* this imbalance matters, starting from the risk of embedding bias in legal decision-making systems and concluding with the underrepresentation of women in the creation and use of legaltech. The underlying causes of the legaltech gender gap – including systemic barriers, cultural norms, and structural issues in both the tech and legal sectors – are investigated. Finally, Priya and Shilpa offer strategies and practical steps for bridging the gap at both the individual and institutional level. AI – when harnessed and adopted thoughtfully – can offer opportunities to advance gender equity within law. If we act early and with intention, AI could be a powerful tool for inclusion and empowerment.

The ability to progress is arguably one of the most critical factors impacting women lawyers' success, as demonstrated by the absence of women in senior roles. It has often been speculated that the reason women leave law is because of either having or caring for their children; however, the data suggest that the primary factor is instead a lack of work–life balance and flexibility in their working environment. In Chapter 4, Herbert Smith Freehills alumna Claire Rason, executive director of Client Talk, explores the concepts of maternal bias, work–life balance, and flexibility through the lens of her own career and research. Prompted by a personal question – "Would I have achieved partnership if I hadn't left the law?" – Claire embarked on a unique experiment. Her research study, *Class of 2002: Women in Law*, traced the career paths of her fellow trainees at Herbert Smith, thereby revealing something startling: despite women making up 57 percent of the cohort, only 23 percent reached the highest levels of the legal profession, compared to 59 percent of their male counterparts. Her findings challenged assumptions about meritocracy and highlighted how organizational culture shapes career outcomes. In this chapter, Claire invites readers to examine the deeper cultural dynamics that continue to hinder gender parity in law firms. She explores the question of whether law firms are an example of a gendered organization, and the ways in which our perceptions of partnership can reveal the unconscious biases we hold. Guidance for both firms and individual practitioners seeking to improve gender parity is offered: firms must challenge traditional working practices, and women lawyers are encouraged to question the narratives they tell themselves and tap into the power of storytelling to initiate change.

Our exploration of women's career progression in law is furthered in Chapter 5, authored by Rachel Khiara, partner at HCR Law, which delves into the ways in which traditional partner-track processes in law firms – from work allocation to criteria for advancement – remain heavily influenced by historic norms shaped by male-dominated settings. These structures perpetuate gender disparities and serve as a barrier to gender equity in leadership, despite data showing that firms with inclusive leadership reap rewards in decision-making, innovation, and profitability. Rachel advocates for practical, structural reforms that decouple partnership eligibility from antiquated norms, such as pressures to conform to certain forms of attire, speech, or demeanor and assumptions equating commitment with extreme hours and limited work–life balance. Such reforms include setting clear, measurable diversity targets; instituting regular reviews of advancement data; and creating formal sponsorship and mentorship programs. When law firms restructure for inclusivity – addressing barriers related to culture, self-promotion, and client pressure – they unlock greater value, performance, and talent retention. Talented women benefit, but so do firms and their clients, strengthening the case for gender equity amidst the current backlash against DEI initiatives.

Chapter 6, authored by Hilda Kwoffie, mentor and founder of The BAME Woman in Law, turns our attention to practical pathways to gender and racial equity in the legal profession. While the profession is slowly becoming more diverse, the reality is stark: women from ethnic minority backgrounds are still up to six times less likely than White men to achieve partnership in large firms and, in law firms across the UK, only 8–9 percent of partners are from ethnic minority backgrounds.[5, 6] Mentorship can aid with development and retention; however, without sponsorship, in which senior leaders in law firms actively advocate for the progression of junior lawyers, too many women of color remain stuck in the pipeline. To combat the tokenism and lack of representation still prominent in the legal profession, Hilda outlines the revolutionary and real-world steps law firms can take to make a tangible impact in achieving racial equity, such as connecting senior staff bonuses, performance reviews, and promotions to measurable outcomes in the retention and progression of women of color and the funding of apprenticeships, scholarships, and outreach designed specifically to support girls and young women of color into legal careers. In these ways, legal institutions can lead with data, accountability, and long-term commitment, lifting the burden from women lawyers of color and reducing the risk of attrition and burnout.

Our intersectional approach continues in Chapter 7 by Yanthé Richardson, president (2024–2025) and non-executive director of the Chartered Institute of Legal Executives and partner at Foot Anstey LLP. The socioeconomic composition of the legal profession remains remarkably static, which can be attributed to systemic barriers, such as decreased access to informal networks for those from disadvantaged socioeconomic backgrounds and recruitment processes that favor traditional qualifications, particularly those from elite universities. This chapter does not ask what women can do better; instead, it challenges the profession to confront systemic exclusion; redesign recruitment, qualification routes, career progression, and firm cultures; and, crucially, to recognize that equity is not charity – it is smart business. Drawing from her own personal and professional experience, Yanthé closely examines the need for access to legal education, training, and practice to be as inclusive as it can be for women and, in particular, those with other intersecting identities or from underprivileged backgrounds. To conclude, Yanthé discusses the practical steps for improving socioeconomic inclusivity in the legal profession to guide firms in attracting and retaining diverse talent.

Chapter 8 – authored by Pam Loch, chief executive officer and founder of the Loch Associates Group – switches our focus to the intersection of neurodiversity and gender within the legal profession, with a focus on the unique experiences of neurodivergent women lawyers. While neurodiversity can bring valuable strengths, such as creativity, hyperfocus, and innovative thinking, it can also present challenges in environments not designed with cognitive diversity in mind and where other people's lack of understanding or acceptance limits potential. For neurodivergent women lawyers, whose cognitive profiles have long been under-recognized and under-supported, the confluence of gendered expectations and neurotypical workplace norms can exact heavy costs in mental health, career progression, and job satisfaction. In this chapter, Pam examines the ways in which traditional legal hiring and working practices can inadvertently exclude neurodivergent women, and how social expectations within the profession compound these barriers. Practical strategies for fostering neuroinclusivity, such as flexible work arrangements, inclusive recruitment, and psychological safety, that will enable neurodivergent women to thrive are discussed, with the ultimate aim of creating a legal profession that values neurodiversity. This will benefit not only affected individuals but, additionally, the wider teams and organizations they contribute to, driving innovation, engagement, and performance.

It is not only young university graduates who want to pursue a career in law; there are many mature aspirant lawyers seeking entry to and progression within the legal profession for a variety of reasons. Career changers often express that law is a calling that they feel no other role can quite satisfy; however, systemic adversities affecting women as they leave young adulthood and approach or enter midlife present what may feel like an insurmountable barrier to the profession. In Chapter 9, Melanie Arens, founder of Later On Lawyers, outlines the challenges faced by women entering the legal profession as a career changer or as they approach midlife, specifically examining the impact of the recent regulatory changes to the admission procedure for solicitors in England and Wales on this demographic. Melanie highlights the potential threat to age and gender-based diversity in the profession based on the qualifying exam datasets and from evidence of current practices emerging from within the legal industry. Drawing from her experience with mature aspiring lawyers as the founder of a supportive online community, Melanie proposes a series of practical recommendations to combat unjustifiable socioeconomic barriers to qualification and offers guidance to prospective career changers in navigating their conversion to law.

Thus far, we have focused almost exclusively on women's career journeys in law firms; however, this changes in Chapter 10, written by Sarah Clark, chief revenue officer at The Legal Director. We are aware that DEI within organizations will falter unless embedded into governance and procurement, rather than being relegated to symbolic gestures or individual champions. Political and corporate pushback, especially in the US and increasingly in the UK, has shifted many DEI efforts from action to appearance. Women, particularly women of color, bear disproportionate burdens when DEI lacks structural support. General counsel (GC) are uniquely placed to safeguard DEI in their position at the intersection of risk, governance, and decision-making, influencing both internal systems and external suppliers. In this chapter, Sarah stresses the importance of systemic reinforcement, independent authority, and consistent market signals, which are essential if DEI is to endure under pressure and scrutiny.

While the focus of this second edition has primarily been change at the systemic level, we would be remiss to neglect offering guidance to women lawyers seeking help navigating the challenges they face during the course of their careers. Rachel Brushfield, founder of EnergiseLegal, shifts our focus in Chapter 11, delving into the possibilities that consultant lawyering offers to women seeking to sidestep the barriers often encountered in private practice, including their disproportionate share of domestic labor and delegation bias in the workplace. Female consultant lawyers and women founders of platform law firms enrich our understanding through their perspectives of the benefits and disadvantages of being a consultant lawyer. For women seeking to pursue this path, Rachel provides insight into the importance of building your career capital and personal branding and establish an in-demand niche and client following, especially in the face of growing competition.

To conclude, in Chapter 12, Jo Brook and Belinda Lester – consultant lawyer and managing director of Lionshead Law, respectively – reinforce the importance of the concept of "amplification". The principle of amplification is simple: find your focus and your platform; establish your professional credentials; listen to what people want and share your views; and find and engage with like-minded people to spread your influence through recommendations, mentoring, and support. Together, Belinda and Jo guide women lawyers through the steps needed to find their voice and use the power of connection to boost their personal and professional profile.

References

1. Solicitors Regulation Authority, "Diversity in law firms' workforce", 3 January 2025. See: https://www.sra.org.uk/sra/equality-diversity/diversity-profession/diverse-legal-profession/
2. International Bar Association Legal Research and Policy Unit, *50:50 by 2030: A longitudinal study into gender disparity in law*, 3 December 2024. See: https://www.ibanet.org/document?id=IBA-Gender-Progress-Report-2024
3. Solicitors Regulation Authority, "Diversity in law firms' workforce", 3 January 2025. See: https://www.sra.org.uk/sra/equality-diversity/diversity-profession/diverse-legal-profession/
4. *Ibid.*
5. Women in the Law UK, "The Business Case For Diversity", 14 February 2018. See: https://www.womeninthelawuk.com/the-business-case-for-diversity/
6. Rose N., "SRA: Men six times more likely to be partners than BAME women", *Legal Futures*, 31 October 2017. See: https://www.legalfutures.co.uk/latest-news/sra-men-six-times-likely-partners-bame-women

About the authors

Melanie Arens is a newly qualified solicitor licensed to practice in England and Wales, with a special interest in family law and international child law. Melanie commenced her legal journey nearly 23 years prior to her qualification by reading law at the University of Southampton, England, before embarking on a career in the local authority youth and children's services. Her pre-qualification professional experience centered on the fields of youth justice, children not in education, and children leaving care, where she carried out both frontline practitioner and managerial positions. In 2009, Melanie completed her master's degree in Human Rights Law at Birkbeck, University of London, gaining insight into international human rights law while interning and consulting in Geneva and Malta before returning to her employment with the UK government.

Melanie spent many years trying to secure a training contract and completed her postgraduate legal practice course and training contract predominately part-time while raising a young family. Further to the challenges she encountered in her qualification journey, Melanie now speaks on issues pertaining to non-linear paths to qualification, working motherhood in law, and wellbeing in the legal profession.

In 2024, Melanie spearheaded a free online community network for mature aspiring career changers to law – Later On Lawyers – which provides inspiration, advice, and support to its members on breaking into the legal profession later in life. Melanie holds regular virtual networking meetings and webinars for the community, drawing on her own extensive network to maximize the group's offering. Melanie's involvement and mentoring of community members has provided her with a unique insight into the challenges specifically faced by career changers and late bloomers in the legal profession.

Melanie spent a short time in private practice post-qualification; at the time of publication, she is due to commence employment with the Ministry of Justice as a legal advisor to the magistrates in the court's family division. She lives on the south coast of England with her husband and two daughters.

Shilpa Bhandarkar is an industry award-winning legal innovator and AI consultant. She advises boards, law firms, and entrepreneurs looking to innovate, scale, and accelerate their growth mandates. Her background is in international law and legaltech; past roles have included partner and head of the client tech and AI team at Linklaters; CEO of CreateiQ; legal network director of Lexoo; and founder and CEO of LetsCoo.

Shilpa has spent the last two years focused on the impact of generative AI on the practice of law, including its potential impact on the gender gap. In collaboration with The Next 100 Years and She Breaks the Law, she led on the publication of the *No Woman Left Behind: Closing the AI Gender Gap* report, published December 2024.

She has been listed as a leading Disruptor in The Lawyer Hot 100 and an individual winner of the TechWomen100 Awards.

Joanne Brook is a solicitor who qualified as the web was launched and has been a legal technologist ever since. She advises innovators across the creative sectors – from software developers and theatre producers to AI and VR developers and artists who distribute NFTs. She focuses on helping clients achieve commercial solutions to previously unencountered legal issues that arise from development and use of their technology. Critically, she protects and licenses their intellectual property rights to ensure business expansion and growth in a fast-paced market. Prior to becoming a legal consultant, she was a partner at a West End law firm and a boutique City law firm. She describes her view of the digital revolution and use of new technologies as being somewhere between sitting, awestruck, in the jumpseat with a supersonic test pilot as the engines roar and calmly evacuating the plane, wearing a parachute and hi-vis, carrying a laptop, and inflating a lifeboat. Between all that, she feels privileged to continue to advise passionate, smart, and more creative people than herself daily.

Joanne is an intellectual property professional expert for LexisNexis and an author of intellectual property and data management precedents for various professional publications. She is a regular contributor to the legal press and lectures on technology and new law.

Rachel Brushfield is The Talent Liberator™® and founder of EnergiseLegal, established 1996. An experienced career strategist and coach with a marketing and brand strategy career heritage, Rachel helps mid-career lawyers to overcome actual and perceived blocks and to create an uplifting breakthrough at major career crossroads. Women lawyers, portfolio careers, personal branding, and consultant lawyers are specialisms.

Content creation projects include career webinars for The Law Society and diversity and inclusion content for LexisNexis. Rachel is a published author in multiple topics, including marketing, career management, professional development, and talent management. A seasoned events professional, Rachel has participated in multiple events for women lawyer networks, including The Law Society UK, The Law Society Northern Ireland, the Society of English and American Lawyers (SEAL), American Women Lawyers in London (AWLL), and Women in the Law (WITL).

As chief revenue officer, **Sarah Clark** leads The Legal Director's commercial strategy, driving brand awareness, lead generation, marketing, and client engagement to support sustained revenue growth. She is responsible for shaping the end-to-end client journey, from market entry through to long-term client relationships, and for ensuring that The Legal Director's proposition remains relevant, differentiated, and client-focused. Sarah plays a pivotal role in enabling The Legal Director's community of experienced general counsel to do their best work – delivering value for clients, building trusted relationships, and enjoying rewarding, fulfilling careers. She brings a strategic, data-led approach to business performance, underpinned by a focus on continuous improvement, a collaborative culture, and client insight.

Rachel Khiara is an experienced partnership lawyer with 25 years' expertise in LLP and partnership law, law firm M&A, private equity investment in the legal sector, and Solicitors Regulation Authority (SRA) regulatory compliance. Currently a partner at HCR Law, she co-leads the firm's Partnerships Group, focusing on non-contentious partnership matters, including governance, structuring, and compliance with SRA rules.

Her expertise extends to advising professional practices (including solicitors, accountants, and architects), investment managers firms, private equity clients, and overseas clients. For many years, Rachel has been recognized in the leading UK legal directories for the depth of her knowledge in partnership practice and her focus on the legal services sector.

Previously, Rachel was a partner at Addleshaw Goddard LLP and counsel at Allen & Overy LLP before founding Khiara Law LLP, a boutique firm specializing in LLP, partnership, and regulatory law. Rachel acts as trusted advisor and provides strategic guidance for senior management boards of law firms. She is passionate about supporting junior lawyers, particularly those with part-time working arrangements and flexible working to accommodate care responsibilities.

Hilda Kwoffie is a solicitor specializing in human rights and civil liberties. She qualified as a solicitor in 2024 after obtaining a first-class degree in LLB Law with European Legal Studies and an MSc LPC in Law, Business and Management. Her postgraduate work focused on diversity and inclusion in the legal sector, reflecting her commitment to diversity and inclusion in the profession.

Hilda is the founder of The BAME Woman in Law, an organization supporting underrepresented women in law through mentorship, skills development, and networking. In recognition of her work, she was named Mentor of the Year at the 2025 Women and Diversity in Law Awards.

An advocate for race, representation, and reform, Hilda has spoken on panels for the Bar Standards Board during Black History Month, delivered a keynote speech at the University of Hull, and participated in discussions at the Houses of Parliament, among other speaking engagements and advocatory initiatives. She continues to champion structural inclusion through public speaking, writing, and mentorship.

Priya Lele is co-founder and chair of She Breaks the Law, a global network of 4,000+ women leaders across 50+ countries reshaping the legal ecosystem. She has over two decades of experience bridging traditional legal practice and digital innovation.

As former director of the EY Legal Transform and Operate practice and senior leader at global law firms, she has extensive experience leading transformation initiatives at law firms and corporate legal departments across the UK, US, EMEA, and Australia.

Passionate about creating inclusive pathways for women's leadership, Priya led the first gender-lensed research into AI adoption in law, publishing *No Woman Left Behind: Closing the AI Gender Gap in Law* (2024) in collaboration with She Breaks the Law, The Next 100 Years, and Linklaters.

A recognized thought leader in legal technology, innovation, and diversity, Priya received the European Women of Legal Tech Award in 2020 and the International Legal Technology Association's Influential Women in Legal Tech Award in 2025.

Upon qualifying, **Belinda Lester** immediately specialized in employment law and worked in various West End and City law firms, becoming a partner in two. Recognizing the uncomfortable tension caused by the need to act swiftly and efficiently to help clients and the need to generate significant fees for firms, as well as realizing that the needs of her professional life and her young family demanded a new way of working, Belinda established Lionshead Law in 2013 as an entirely virtual law firm. With a clear desk and a keen understanding of social media engagement, Belinda built the firm using various digital platforms to secure and deliver work remotely. Addressing the incongruity of hourly rates, and free from the overhead of London offices, Lionshead Law initially worked on fixed fees and retainers only while building a network of self-employed senior consultant lawyers, who are experts in their fields and prepared take a high percentage on billing rather than waiting for partners to take their cut and hope for an annual bonus or a pay raise.

Belinda is known as a tough negotiator and fearsome litigator, and is frequently commended by her clients for being clear, concise, practical, and solution-focused while simultaneously being empathetic and supportive. She is a member of the Employment Lawyers' Association and frequent contributor to professional press and media on the subject of employment law matters.

Pam Loch is a dual-qualified solicitor who established Loch Associates Group in 2007 to respond to the need for bespoke solutions to the challenges facing organizations as they grow. Today, Loch Associates Group is an award-winning legal, HR, training, and wellbeing and mediation organization, with the aim of creating responsible, high-performing, and progressive businesses. As well as being the driving force behind the business, Pam has also been a specialist, award-winning solicitor for over 20 years, writing thought-leading articles and book chapters, as well as acting as a seasoned commentator for television and radio.

For the last 14 years, Pam has been ranked as a leading solicitor in employment law in the Legal 500's and Chambers and Partners' legal guides, with Loch Law (part of the Loch Associates Group) also being ranked as a leading firm. Loch Law is also recognized as a top 250 employment law firm by *The Times*. Her passion for finding solutions to help businesses manage and look after their people is reflected in the development and success of the businesses across the Loch Associates Group.

Claire Rason is an accredited coach (as a senior practitioner by the European Mentoring and Coaching Council), founder of Client Talk, and co-founder of B-Contagious. A former practicing solicitor, she has worked in and alongside professional services firms for over two decades. In her work as a team coach, Claire raises awareness of the impact bias, so that teams can collaborate more effectively and inclusively. She is passionate about embedding active listening in firms to drive meaningful change. Claire is a strong advocate for gender parity at partnership level and has conducted research into the barriers women face in reaching senior roles. Her report, *Class of 2002: Women in Law*, is available to download for free on the Client Talk website. She is co-author of books on women in business development and coaching, and hosts the Lawyer's Coach podcast.

Yanthé Richardson is an equity partner at growing national top 100 law firm Foot Anstey LLP, and was the president of the Chartered Institute of Legal Executives (CILEX) between 2024–2025. Her career in law began as a school leaver in 2003. She trained vocationally via CILEX Law School, initially qualifying in family law. She practiced at Josiah–Lake Gardiner LLP in London before re-specializing in property and joining Foot Anstey in 2014. With a specialism in new-build and affordable housing, Yanthé now leads teams that act for both developers/registered providers and buyers. Sitting on the Land Registry Advisory Council and the Digital Property Market Steering Group, and acting as the lawyer representative on the New Homes Quality Board's Code Review Council, she is known as an industry expert in new-build housing matters.

Yanthé was recognized in Obelisk's 2024 *Women Who Will* report: "Yanthé's commitment to accessible legal education and her leadership within CILEX have established her as a significant advocate for social mobility in law. Her achievements underscore her impact as a transformative figure in the legal profession." She is passionate about the importance of increasing socioeconomic diversity in the legal profession.

Rachel Spink is a partner at Gunnercooke LLP and an employment lawyer with over 20 years' experience. Rachel represents clients in UK Employment Tribunal and High Court litigation and advises companies and individuals on resolving complex workplace disputes.

Rachel is the founder of Female Lawyers' Club, a membership and career development platform that supports women in law to design careers on their own terms, with higher pay, greater autonomy, and a sustainable work–life balance. Through expert-led masterclasses, strategic networking, and practical tools, the Club empowers members to grow in confidence, build resilience, and thrive professionally and personally.

Rachel regularly writes about gender equity, inclusive leadership, and the future of legal careers, and is passionate about reshaping the legal profession to better support the progression and wellbeing of women.

Brie Stevens-Hoare KC is a client-focused barrister, practicing from Gatehouse Chambers. Brie specializes in property disputes, focusing in particular on real property, property development, and the more commercial aspects of property work. In addition, she has developed a strong reputation for her contentious probate work, which frequently involves property issues.

Brie is ranked in Band 1 as a leading King's Counsel in real estate in the 2025 editions of both the Legal 500 and Chambers and Partners' legal guides, and is also ranked for her contentious probate work and as a mediator.

Brie served as a Judicial Appointments Commissioner (2018–2024). She is Lincoln's Inn's Co-Convenor of the Inns of Court Women's Alliance and has worked with the Bar Council on the impact of the menopause. Brie is also a founding member of the Bar's LGBTQIA+ network, FreeBar.

Chapter 1: Authenticity and identity in law: building inclusive legal workplaces through intersectionality

By Brie Stevens-Hoare KC, barrister, Gatehouse Chambers

The term "intersectionality" was first used by the Black feminist legal academic Professor Kimberlé Crenshaw, who argued that existing frameworks for understanding and addressing discrimination through the law, which tended to focus on or address one characteristic at a time, were inadequate.[1] She described how, in instances where a person or group identify with more than one characteristic, such as race and gender, the overlapping impact of inequalities relating to each characteristic can create a palimpsest of discrimination. Intersectionality invites us to understand and address the impact of inequalities through a more complex and nuanced lens, looking beyond the individual strands of diversity into the experience of real people and groups with multiple points of difference that drive the inequality and/or discrimination they experience.

An example in the legal sector today, which draws on Crenshaw's intersection between race and gender, is the income gap experienced by female lawyers from minority ethnic backgrounds. There has been a focus on addressing gender disparity for many years. However, the statistics show that, despite improved representation, a persistent income gap across all contexts in which lawyers work: private practice, corporate sector, public sector, and the judiciary, with slow progress being made.[2]

More recently, the analysis of demographic, employment, and financial data from the legal profession has included an intersectional approach. The picture is not a pretty one: as an example, the latest data for the Bar of England and Wales ("the Bar") from the Bar Standards Board demonstrates that, on average:

- Female barristers' incomes are 57 percent that of their male counterparts;
- Barristers from minority ethnic backgrounds have an income that is 74 percent that of their White counterparts' income; and
- The incomes of female barristers from minority ethnic backgrounds

> are 47 percent of those of White male barristers, the highest-earning group at the Bar.[3]

Without an intersectional approach to the income data, a real understanding of the experiences and incomes of female barristers from minority ethnic backgrounds could not be attained. It would instead appear that they are only impacted by the 57 percent lower earning potential faced by female barristers.

A real focus on the potentially transformational value of an intersectional approach to any efforts to address inequality and/or discrimination related to certain characteristics is more recent. It was summarized very effectively by associate professor Shreya Atrey, a legal academic with a focus on the intersection of feminist theory and disability law. Atrey described the value of intersectionality as follows:

> *"[Intersectionality] helps [us to] understand the structure and dynamic consequences of the interaction between multiple forms of disadvantage based on race, sex, gender, disability, class, age, caste, religion, sexual orientation, region, etc. In helping to understand this complexity, it opens up ways to address the disadvantage associated with it."*[4, 5]

This chapter considers the ways in which the concept of intersectionality, beyond its value in revealing the efficacy (or otherwise) of discrimination law, can enhance efforts to make legal practice inclusive for all lawyers working within it – across all strands of diversity. At the heart of an intersectional perspective is the understanding that people and groups may be disadvantaged by multiple characteristics or experiences in differing ways. The specific impacts of each will vary, and how an individual responds to those impacts will differ. The overall effects include some outcomes relating to representation, selection, income, and progression in the legal professions that most will be familiar with. However, we cannot truly identify or understand the changes we must collectively make until we look at and take account of all relevant characteristics and experiences, whether they operate to disadvantage and/or advantage an individual or group.

Intersectionality: shared struggles or diverse realities?

By its nature, an intersectional perspective highlights and considers the differences between groups of people. Not all women are equal; they do not have a single experience or face the same range of challenges or disadvantages. The barristers' income data cited above demonstrate very clearly one aspect in which the experience of women from minority ethnic backgrounds is demonstrably worse than White women in the same profession.

In the effort to understand the structures that disadvantage different people, and the variety of challenges and barriers they face, a good starting point may be consideration of the fundamental differences between the characteristics and experience we might need to take into account. When thinking about the traditional protected characteristics in discrimination law, it is apparent that they are not all the same in nature. Some are characteristics that everyone possesses, such as race, sex, age, and so on. In terms of those characteristics, the disadvantaged experience is borne from a hierarchy: disadvantage is created in societies or situations in which a particular sex, race, or age is considered lesser or does not represent the dominant or "prized" version of that characteristic. Such societies are designed by and for those with the dominant or "prized" characteristics, creating structural inequality and barriers. The experience of the disadvantaged individual within such societies can be a mix of anger, an overwhelming sense of injustice and/or impotence, and/or an internalization of the belief that they are less valuable and valued. Both the reality of inequality and the internalization of that reality contribute to the lived experience of disadvantage that any individual facing discrimination, disadvantage, or barriers must navigate.

Some characteristics are only possessed by part of the population, such as disability or pregnancy; in some cases, those who demonstrate or identify with those characteristics may only do so temporarily. Those characteristics tend to result in an association with being particularly vulnerable or less able or valuable, due to the simple fact of – and for the duration of – that condition or state of being. For those who possess such a characteristic for only a period of their life, experiencing the change in how they are perceived or treated adds yet another dimension to navigate. The change may be acute and difficult to adjust to, but it may also provide insight, which can inform the individual's ability to challenge the disadvantages imposed by society.

Another apparent difference between characteristics is how visible they are to those around us. Humans tend to believe that they can correctly identify the sex, gender, race, and even the age of those around them. Gender and/or race are probably the characteristics we can most often correctly identify. Most women, and many people from an ethnic minority background, have little or no control over being perceived as their gender or race. For some, this experience manifests as frequent mischaracterization by others, which creates its own challenges. The consequence of visible characteristics (even if wrongly identified by others) is the inability of the individual to avoid the structural disadvantages and/or barriers that flow from being understood to possess that particular characteristic by those around you – day in and day out.

Other characteristics – such as sexual orientation, religion, or some disabilities – may not be as readily apparent to others, and many individuals may have the option of "invisibility". The impact of deciding (or being compelled to decide) to conceal part of your identity can be complex and create its own barriers and challenges.[6] As an example, history is full of those who choose – for good reason – to conceal their sexual orientation. Some internalize homophobia, and others may find themselves judged for having "deceived" those around them if they finally make a decision to live authentically. When society stigmatizes a characteristic, invisibility may be the sensible – even life-saving – choice, which can bring a lot of advantages. However, a price is often paid for this concealment, which may leave individuals vulnerable to psychological or physical harm and/or extortion if discovered. Refusal to accept one's true identity privately or publicly can also lead to poor mental health outcomes.[7]

Understanding inclusion and intersectionality through diverse lived experiences

Race and legal practice: a diverse reality

In recent years, the degree of focus on inequality amongst lawyers by reason of race has significantly intensified. However, the application of the approach used to identify and seek to address gender inequality was soon shown to be inadequate when it came to tackling racial discrimination. Examining and addressing racial inequality involves the consideration of many different backgrounds, perspectives, and experiences, where disparities and their drivers differ, sometimes very significantly. Approaching the existent barriers as though lawyers from minority ethnic backgrounds were one group with a common experience masks the truth: the degree of disparity varies between different racial groups, as do experiences of discrimination.

Consideration of the ways in which the most basic racial stereotypes might play out for lawyers in practice is a very quick and easy way to identify the need to look beyond the label of Black, Asian and minority ethnic (BAME) in the same way that one must look beyond the categorization of "female" as one group with a single common experience. Stereotypes often drive the expectation others have of individual members of a group. As such, even senior lawyers seeking to be a positive influence may impose racially driven expectations on an individual, which affect the opportunities they are offered and obscure their real strengths and weakness. Stereotypes around hardworking and enterprising South Asian communities, or those from East Asian backgrounds being "good with numbers", may encourage the perception that individuals from these groups may be suited to more commercial work. Similarly, the idea that a Black person must have come from a deprived area, or the adultification of Black people, can lead to the assumption they will be interested in addressing crime and depravation, rather than commercial or Chancery work, and that they are inured to the harmful impact of dealing with the traumatic aspects of that work.

As a more nuanced approach is adopted, the impacts of inequality on lawyers from different racial groups have begun to be more widely understood. A report on the experience of Black barristers at the specialist Bar in England and Wales concluded:

> *"The substantive evidence gathered through the questionnaires and roundtables deserves careful scrutiny and vividly illustrates some of the cultural hurdles and barriers faced by Black barristers. The evidence gathered by the BIG Committee's work points to a culture experienced by Black barristers characterized by profound levels of isolation, dislocation, and not belonging. The evidence also points to high levels of race and/or ethnicity-related behaviors, including banter, bullying, and/or discrimination/bias. Surprisingly and disappointingly high proportions of those who responded to the survey (of all ethnicities) reported direct experience and/or witnessing and/or awareness of such behaviors. A lack of support, particularly from senior barristers and clerks/practice managers, was also reported."*[8]

The evidence gathered in this report demonstrates the acutely damaging effect being easily identified as coming from a particular group and the experience of being "the only one" can have. That can result in the dissonant combination of being both "hypervisible", judged as a representative of your group, while simultaneously being unseen by the dominant culture and those around you, feeling profoundly alone and bearing the heavy weight of those expectations.

At a high level, the very human experience of not belonging; not being seen or respected for who we are as individuals; being prejudged by reference to stereotypical ideas and expectations of our group; and fearing that our failure (or the failure of other women) will be treated as the failure of our group is familiar for many women lawyers. Indeed, the emerging work around racial discrimination in the legal professions helps to show that – at a macro level – the experience of inequality resonates with the core parts of our collective humanity. There is much that lawyers from each group share, and those who occupy multiple groups may understand that particularly acutely. Whilst women as a whole are not a minority, there is a lot of common ground and mutual interest in the efforts to address gender and racial inequalities. Moreover, working to understand and address racial equalities can give new or deeper insights into the mechanisms of gender inequality. Understanding those mechanisms and how they impact individuals from ethnic minority groups can help women to better understand the experience of those who share their gender, but not their race. That is a good starting point for ensuring that all work on gender equality takes account of the rich diversity that exists within the group that is female lawyers.

Sexuality, gender identity, and the legal professions

The LGBTQ+ community, by definition, is an inclusive community of people with varied characteristics and experiences. For instance, many of the experiences of those who are bisexual or pansexual are very different from those lesbians and gay men whose attraction is confined to one gender. The characteristics and experiences of transgender people, particularly at the time of writing, are different yet again. Anyone who has watched the film Pride will have some insight into what that inclusive community provides to its membership as a counterpoint to the discrimination, stigmatization, and harassment they experience. The film contains clear examples of the LGBTQ+ community working to find strength in their shared or common experience, rather than division in their differences. The protagonists demonstrate allyship with the miners, as well as with each other, challenging stereotypes and negative language by adopting them with joy and humor and reclaiming words such as "queer", drawing on that sense of community and shared challenges to withstand stigma and direct attacks with resilience and pride, uplifting itself with celebration and joy along the way.

The LGBTQ+ community has had to be honest with itself and work to tackle racism and transphobia from within, and continues to do so.

Nevertheless, even today, when the public discourse around trans people is so negative, the vast majority of the LGBTQ+ community is supportive of trans people as the community works to challenge the same narratives and attacks that gay men and lesbians faced decades ago.[9] The current experience of both the international and UK LGBTQ+ community is a good reminder that progress can be halted or regress. A lesson learnt for all groups is that maintaining a strong, cohesive community that remains vigilant and conscious of its own prejudices is crucial, as progress is not fixed in stone. Maintaining that strong community involves an inclusive approach to embracing diversity from within, demonstrating that the work on gender equality is focused on the experience of all women – not just those (even if it is the largest part of the group) for whom progress comes first.

The allyship of gay men with women is another key point demonstrated by the LGBTQ+ experience. The contribution and value of straight allies to the progress made over recent decades is known and understood. That allyship can work both ways. For instance, gay men are often present at the table when women are discussed. In that context, they have an opportunity and the agency to challenge harmful, inaccurate, and unfair narratives, whether they relate to individual women or to women as a group. In instances where men prefer to listen to men, a gay man may be a powerful advocate. Gay men can often articulate the experience of exclusion or not sharing interests with the dominant group and convey how that impacts people to members of the dominant group in a way that a woman often cannot.

A powerful example of a gay male ally for women in the legal professions is Daniel Winterfelt, who founded InterLaw. The work being undertaken by the InterLaw Diversity Forum to address gender, race, and disability in law as it stands is extensive, targeted, constructive, often celebratory, and very effective.[10] InterLaw began as an LGBTQ+ lawyers network founded by Daniel, a gay man. The part of its ethos that includes celebration, pride, and joy as tools to tackle inequality and adversity resonates deeply with the wider LGBTQ+ community's approach. InterLaw's work exemplifies the additional power and effectiveness of being inclusive and intersectional.

Legal work and neurodivergent identities

In the law, as in society, a proper focus on neurodiversity and inequality is relatively new. A particularly interesting aspect of current efforts relating to neurodiversity in legal practice is that many of the initiatives have been spearheaded by junior lawyers and new entrants to the profession. The call for an understanding of and respect for the particular skills and ways of thinking that neurodiverse people can bring, which have proved beneficial in certain aspects of legal work, is a refreshingly constructive starting point to tackle inequality. Work on addressing gender discrimination has long involved making the business case for equality, attempting to persuade and advocate for the proper engagement of female talent. The message from the neurodiverse legal community is more positive and unabashed: it states clearly that it has a lot to offer. Neurodiverse individuals have valuable, highly developed skills that can be overlooked or inhibited by environments that do not understand them. Therefore, if the barriers were only removed, those talents would be given the space to flourish; through small accommodations, neurodiverse lawyers can enjoy a less challenging professional life.

Looking to the neurodiverse lawyer community is a very valuable reminder to bring those who are new to the profession into the work from an early stage. Seniority is not a prerequisite for those who want to make change. Through early engagement and inclusion, young women beginning their careers in the profession may have the opportunity to be bolder in their message and battle less with imposter syndrome and the internalization of the outdated and disproven stereotypes that my generation navigated for too long.

Barriers and bias: socioeconomic status and class in the legal sector

In the UK, social class – and its connection to the law and the legal profession – is centuries-old. A look around many legal institutions confirms how embedded, historic, and established class culture is to the profession. In this context, "social class" is a reference to the complex aspects of British people's identity related to their social status and standing. Social class, which is related to historic, cultural, and familial context, is always hard to quantify but nevertheless remains a significant part of British society and its structuring of power and influence. The UK's conception of social class is related to – but does not correlate with – socioeconomic status, which is a quantitative measure based on income, education, and occupation.[11] Socioeconomic status, without the added layer of class, is likely to be more relevant in other countries or contexts.

The reality is that a person's socioeconomic background intersects with other characteristics. The relationship between individuals' socioeconomic status and access to health and social care services can be particularly relevant in the context of disability and neurodiversity. For instance, recognition in the legal professions of the inequality associated with being a child under the care of social services, without good access to opportunities, is only just beginning to surface. Addressing socioeconomic disparity is inclusive work, given the relationship it has with other strands of diversity. For instance, there is an intimate connection between race and socioeconomic factors or perceived socioeconomic status. There are statistically significant differences in socioeconomic status between different ethnic groups in both the UK and the US.[12, 13] The connection goes further, thanks to the erroneous perception that anyone from a minority ethnic group comes from a disadvantaged socioeconomic background. Understanding how those connections operate contributes to efforts to tackle discrimination related to race and to socioeconomic factors within the legal professions.

Manifestations of socioeconomic disparity appear in a person's educational background and their access to long-established networks with deep connections to the legal professions. Those manifestations are a factor in gender inequality: even female lawyers from wealthy backgrounds cannot attend the prestigious boys' schools, such as Eton or Harrow, and – until as recently as 2024 – were not allowed to be members of the Garrick Club, one of the oldest and most exclusive private members' clubs in the world, which has long been associated with the legal profession.

Whilst some of those women who broke glass ceilings in the law had the benefit of coming from wealthy families with pre-existing connections to the law, others did not. With women representing more than 50 percent of those entering the legal professions, efforts to address gender inequality that do not include socioeconomic inequality do a disservice to many of those women. Addressing the disparity between women from non-privileged backgrounds and those joining the profession with the advantage of cultural capital and connections and an intimate knowledge of and comfort in that culture will inevitably assist the progress of women's equality in legal practice.

Understanding barriers for women in law: an intersectional perspective

An intersectional approach to addressing gender equality in the legal professions enables an understanding of the barriers that hinder different groups of women lawyers. For instance, recognizing that the barriers facing disabled women will vary from those hindering the progress of others, and that some shared barriers will affect those disabled women differently, improves our understanding of what needs to change for the benefit of all. Having a better grasp of the range of barriers and the mechanisms by which they disadvantage people can help us to change processes and ways of working – not just to remove these barriers for particular demographics, but to create flexible, inclusive processes or cultures to reduce disparities for all women in the law.

To take an example in relation to recruitment criteria, there was a time when attendance of certain educational institutions was taken as a proxy for good intellect. Recognition of gendered limits on access to those institutions and a shift to a focus on educational achievement overall increased fairness and access to some female talent. A further, more intersectional understanding that better-resourced education contributes to better exam results, and that those from a disadvantaged socioeconomic background may not have had the luxury of well-resourced schools – or, indeed, the necessary equipment; the time and space to study; private tuition; or others who could support their learning – will encourage a move towards incorporating tools that assess the intellectual ability of the individual, rather than placing reliance on exam results as a reliable proxy for their capability. Factoring in other considerations, such as a person's first language or any neurodiversity they may have, will push those seeking to recruit high-performing individuals to go in search of selection tools that allow direct testing of their abilities, with a contextual adjustment to enable their raw skills and future potential to be considered.

It is only by looking at the barriers which affect all women, and those that affect some women, that we can take the drive for gender equality beyond the point we have reached thus far. For a long time, discussions about gender equality in the law focused primarily on the impact of motherhood. However, anecdotal experience and hard data suggest women who do not have children experience very similar inequalities. That is perhaps most vividly demonstrated when reviewing gender income gap data, which reveal that the inequality between men and women starts from the beginning of female lawyers' careers, at a point when few will have had children.[14] InterLaw's intersectional research on pay gaps in law firms, taking gender and sexual orientation into consideration, points to gay women – who, historically, are less likely to have had children – being noticeably less disadvantaged than their straight counterparts but who are, nevertheless, significantly disadvantaged when compared to gay and straight men.[15] Whilst the perception that all women are likely to become mothers affects those women who ultimately do not, that does not mean that the potential women have for motherhood is the only reason for inequality. If motherhood was the only contributing factor, the current experience of out gay women and older women (who are either known to be child-free or to have already had their children) should be free of disadvantage and barriers. Neither the data discussed above nor anecdotal experience accord with that idea. That leads us to the realization that motherhood is not the only driver of inequality and encourages a wider focus. The impact of gendered expectations when it comes to certain behaviors and characteristics comes into view: men are assertive; ruthlessness is good; however, women who are aggressive and ruthlessness are bad. The intersection with race in regard to those expectations further highlights some of their differing and more extreme impact on female lawyers from minority ethnic backgrounds, who experience greater disparities than White women. Moreover, consideration of socioeconomic factors, including the old boys' network, can highlight and inform an appreciation of the disparity in mentoring and sponsoring opportunities that are offered to men and women.

The deeper and more comprehensive an understanding we have of the barriers that women (which means some – as well as all – women) face, the more targeted and effective efforts to achieve gender equality can be. Gender equality simply cannot exist unless and until the barriers that affect any groups of women are addressed. If we only target what we believe affects all women, many barriers will remain, and only some women will achieve equality.

The risks of intersectionality

An intersectional approach requires a focus on difference; however, that focus needs to be a part of the story, rather than its entirety, which can result in division. An intersectional approach is not about eliminating difference; it is about identifying, acknowledging, and removing differing barriers and/or the varying heights and breadths of shared barriers. Seeking to make all women's experience the same, and encouraging assimilation as means of navigating around different barriers, is the antithesis of intersectional and inclusive work. Similarly, since the value of intersectionality is a comprehensive change that benefits all women lawyers, a singular focus on women's other overlapping characteristics is counterproductive.

It is an inevitability that no one fully understands everyone else's experience and, try as we might, we can never truly stand in another person's shoes. The risk of getting it wrong is, therefore, high. Managing those errors, missteps, and the occasions offence is caused is difficult, tiring, and sometimes painful. However, ensuring that initiatives and activity address shared – as well as differing – experience is possible. This requires an openness to listen to a range of voices and revisit initial decisions; an understanding that some things are beyond your experience; and an acknowledgement that learning from others is essential, as is being willing to constantly revise your approach to accommodate difference. Additionally, the humility to identify and acknowledge responsibility when an omission or misstep occurs is critical.

Applying intersectionality: tools and requirements for inclusive practice

Intersectional and inclusive perspectives allow us to more deeply understand what needs to change. It increases the number of those we can work in collaboration with when seeking gender equality, as well as opening us up to incredible allies. When working to create inclusive workplaces and professions that benefit all women, we can move beyond addressing the obvious barriers to those that are less evident and more nuanced and embedded, achieving systemic change that raises up other disadvantaged groups.

Knowledge; increased interest in the outcome; and increased beneficiaries make for a powerful and sustainable effort. The essential behaviors to enable our collective, inclusive, intersectional effort are:

- An openness to difference;
- Active listening;
- An acknowledgment that there will be missteps and mistakes;
- Humility when those happen;
- Flexibility and a willingness to revisit and adjust;
- Resilience; and
- A sense of humor.

The reward is getting ever closer to gender equality, which cannot come quickly enough.

References

1 Crenshaw K., "Demarginalizing the intersection of race and sex: A Black feminist critique of antidiscrimination doctrine, feminist theory and antiracist politics", *University of Chicago Legal Forum*, 1989, volume 1, pp. 139–167

2 International Bar Association, *50:50 by 2030: A longitudinal study into gender disparity in law*, 2022. See: www.ibanet.org/document?id=IBA-Gender-Disparity-Report-England-and-Wales-2022

3 Bar Standards Board, "Bar Standards Board report shows persistent income gaps by gender and ethnicity at the Bar", 1 July 2025. See:

www.barstandardsboard.org.uk/resources/resource-library/bar-standards-board-report-shows-persistent-income-gaps-by-gender-and-ethnicity-at-the-bar.html
4 Atrey S., *Intersectional Discrimination*, Oxford: Oxford University Press; 2019.
5 Alessi NP, "Intersectionality as a legal concept? Applications and implications of the notion (within and) beyond non-discrimination law", *BioLaw*, 2025, volume 1, pp. 475–505. http://dx.doi.org/10.15168/2284-4503-3503
6 Lingsom S., "Invisible Impairments: Dilemmas of Concealment and Disclosure", *Scandinavian Journal of Disability Research*, 2008, volume 10, issue 1, pp. 2–16. https://doi.org/10.1080/15017410701391567
7 Moagi M.M., van Der Wath A.E., Jiyane P.M., and Rikhotso R.S., "Mental health challenges of lesbian, gay, bisexual and transgender people: An integrated literature review", *Health SA*, 2021, volume 26, p. 1487. https://doi.org/10.4102/hsag.v26i0.1487
8 Jinadu A.L., Lee K., Pryce G., Richmond J., and Stevens-Hoare B., *"The Specialist Commercial Bar & Black Inclusion – First Steps"*, The Commercial Bar Association, April 2022. See: https://www.combar.com/news/the-specialist-commercial-bar-black-inclusion-first-steps/
9 Just Like Us, *The impact of school, home and coronavirus on LGBT+ young people*, June 2021. See: https://justlikeus.org/wp-content/uploads/2021/11/Just-Like-Us-2021-report-Growing-Up-LGBT.pdf
10 InterLaw Diversity Forum, "What We Do", September 2025. See: https://www.interlawdiversityforum.org/what-we-do
11 National Centre for Social Research, "40 years of British Social Attitudes: Class identity and awareness still matter", 21 September 2023. See: https://natcen.ac.uk/news/40-years-british-social-attitudes-class-identity-and-awareness-still-matter
12 Office for National Statistics, "UK population by ethnicity: Socioeconomic status", 13 June 2025. See: https://www.ethnicity-facts-figures.service.gov.uk/uk-population-by-ethnicity/demographics/socioeconomic-status/latest/
13 Noël R.A., "Race, Economics, and Social Status", US Bureau of Labor Statistics, May 2018. See: https://www.bls.gov/spotlight/2018/race-economics-and-social-status/home.htm
14 Bar Council, "Mind the early gender earnings gap at the Bar – new research from the Bar Council", 23 April 2024. See: https://www.barcouncil.org.uk/resource/mind-the-early-gender-earnings-gap-at-the-bar-new-research-from-the-bar-council.html
15 InterLaw Diversity Forum, "LGBT+ Factsheet: Key findings from the 2021 report, Career Progression Report in the Legal Sector", 2021. See: https://www.interlawdiversityforum.org/_files/ugd/5aa06e_b8150387ca1243418743b2b75f675414.pdf

Chapter 2:
Who made the rules? Dismantling gendered leadership in law

By Rachel Spink, founder, Female Lawyers' Club

I still remember the phone call. A few days earlier, I had given what I thought was a strong presentation to the promotion committee. I had explained the years I had spent pursuing a new client: a huge organization which would be a prestigious client for the firm. I had built the relationship from the ground up: offering training, meeting with multiple stakeholders, and following up consistently. Eventually, after years of effort, they had sent us work. It was a significant win.

At the time, all the partners in my department were men. Any new opportunities that came in were passed directly to them. If you weren't already a partner, you had to generate new work on your own and, in an environment where the clients rarely changed legal providers, that wasn't easy. However, I had found a way. So, when the call came from a male partner to discuss the outcome, I was expecting congratulations; instead, I got a warning. "They were impressed," he said. "But there was some concern that you didn't credit others in the department. It came across as though you did it all yourself."

The thing was – I had done it myself. Not because I was determined to go it alone, but because there had been no guidance, no sharing of opportunities, and very little support. In that firm, if you weren't already a partner, you were on your own. Yet, somehow, the very qualities I needed to demonstrate – independence and proactivity – were now being held against me. I was eventually promoted, but only after a (male) partner vouched for me. It was not my results that were questioned, but the way I had achieved them. I was told I had not sufficiently acknowledged the role of teamwork in my success. The irony was hard to ignore: I was criticized for not demonstrating teamwork by people who had themselves become partners in a system that rewarded individualism and did not promote the sharing of opportunities or supporting others on the way up.

It was the first time I saw it clearly: the double-bind. In many law firms, traits like assertiveness, ambition, and independence are celebrated... when demonstrated by men. However, when women display the same behaviors, they risk being labeled difficult, ungrateful, arrogant, or uncollaborative. Had I been a man, I suspect the story would have been different. The narrative would have been: he's got drive; he takes initiative; he's a leader. Instead, my competence was a cause for concern.

At the time, I thought it was just me. Only later, after years of speaking with other women lawyers, did I see the pattern. I have since heard countless stories from women who were told they were too confident, too direct, too ambitious... and who struggled to get promoted as a result. This chapter includes some of those stories, because they reveal the hidden cost of how we currently define leadership, but it does not end there, because this is not just about fairness – it is about effectiveness. If the current model of legal leadership punishes women for demonstrating characteristics that get men promoted, we must ask: is the model itself broken?

In the legal profession, we have long viewed leadership through a narrow and deeply gendered lens; one that overvalues traits like dominance, control, and visibility, and undervalues others such as emotional intelligence, collaboration, and humility. These latter traits are often gendered as "feminine" and are qualities that many women already bring to the table but are rarely rewarded for. Research explored later in this chapter shows that these traits are just as – if not more so – critical to sustainable, high-performing teams than the characteristics traditionally valued in the legal profession. This chapter explores the ways in which our current leadership frameworks exclude not only people, but potential. While it begins with my story, it reflects the collective experience of many women in law and invites us all to examine what leadership really means today. Through research, real-world examples, and conversations with law firm leaders, we will ask:

- What if the traits that make great leaders have been present – but undervalued – in the legal profession because they are seen as "feminine"?
- What might law look like if we embraced a fuller, fairer, and more effective definition of leadership?
- How do we redesign our systems so that the people best equipped to lead are not pushed out simply because they don't conform to outdated, masculine-coded models of leadership?

By continuing to exalt a narrow and dated view of leadership, the legal profession has not just limited individual careers – it has also compromised the performance, profitability, and long-term sustainability of legal organizations themselves.

Where are the women?

Despite years of progress in gender equality and diversity initiatives, women remain significantly underrepresented in senior legal leadership roles, particularly in the UK and US.

In the UK, women make up over half of all solicitors (53 percent, according to the Solicitors Regulation Authority), yet only 37 percent of partners in law firms; the percentage drops further at the equity level and among larger firms.[1] Across the Atlantic, women account for just 24 percent of equity partners in US law firms, according to the National Association for Law Placement.[2] For women of color, the numbers are even starker: in 2024, women lawyers of color made up only 5 percent of all partners, and only about 3percent of equity partners in US firms.[3,4]

The result is not just a visibility gap – it is also a power and pay gap. The lack of women in senior roles contributes directly to the persistent gender pay gap in the legal profession.

In 2024, leading UK firms continued to report mean gender pay gaps of 11–18 percent, with median gaps as high as 40 percent in some cases.[5,6] These figures reflect more than just unequal pay: they reveal a structural imbalance in who holds the most senior, highest-paid positions.

This underrepresentation also shapes culture. Without diverse voices at the top, law firms risk reinforcing narrow, traditional models of success, often rooted in outdated assumptions about what a leader looks and sounds like. In the discussion that follows, we will look at the origins of these ideas: how leadership came to be gendered; what the research shows; and how that legacy continues to shape women's experiences in law today.

The gendered lens of leadership: what the research shows

The "think manager, think male" phenomenon

Leadership has long been associated with traditionally "masculine" traits, such as dominance, rationality, independence and assertiveness. While this reflects the lived experience of many women in law, psychologist Virginia Schein's landmark research in the early 1970s was the first to provide empirical evidence that leadership is unconsciously "coded" as male.[7] In this context, "coded" means that certain traits or behaviors are socially associated with a particular gender – not because they are inherently male or female, but because of longstanding cultural assumptions about what men and women are like and how they behave.

In her 1973 study, Schein asked participants in the US to rate how well a range of 92 personality characteristics described one of three target groups: men in general; women in general; or a successful middle manager. The traits ranged from assertive, competitive, and objective to warm, helpful, and emotional. The results revealed a striking pattern: when participants were asked to describe a successful *manager*, the traits they chose – such as assertiveness, independence, self-confidence, competitiveness, and objectivity – closely aligned with those they associated with men. In contrast, traits more often attributed to women – such as sensitivity, warmth, helpfulness, and emotionality – were not seen to match the defining characteristics of effective managers. In other words, participants tended to equate being a good manager with being male. This phenomenon became known as the "think manager, think male" effect.

In 2001, Schein replicated the study across the UK, Germany, China, and Japan and found similar bias: traits seen as "managerial" continued to match male-coded characteristics, confirming that leadership remains deeply masculinized across cultures and industries.[8]

Masculine-coded vs feminine-coded traits

To understand how leadership came to be perceived as masculine, we need to look more closely at the traits society tends to associate with each gender. Over decades of research in psychology, management, and gender studies, scholars have consistently found that certain traits are socially labeled as "masculine" or "feminine," and that these labels impact our perceptions of who is fit to lead.[9]

Traits typically seen as masculine, and therefore more aligned with traditional leadership norms, include:

- Assertiveness;
- Decisiveness;
- Independence;
- Competitiveness;
- Rationality over emotion;
- Risk-taking; and
- Authoritativeness.

By contrast, feminine-coded traits tend to include:

- Empathy;
- Collaboration;
- Supportiveness;
- Adaptability;
- Compassion;
- Emotional intelligence; and
- Relationship-building.

These categories are not biologically determined; they are shaped by cultural expectations. Research has shown that these stereotypes create prescriptive norms: men are expected to be strong, decisive, and independent, whereas women are expected to be nurturing, cooperative, and accommodating.[10] When individuals diverge from these expectations, particularly in high-status professions like law, they can be penalized, as I found reflected in the experience I shared at the beginning of this chapter. In the legal profession, traits like credibility, confidence, and control are often seen as essential for leadership. As a result, the qualities many women lead with, or simply feel more comfortable expressing, can be viewed as inadequate, or even as weaknesses. This creates a subtle but continuous pressure to adopt a more traditionally "masculine" leadership style, even when it feels inauthentic or unsustainable. The result is a no-win situation for many women in law, and creates a double-bind when they try to lead.

The double-bind dilemma

When leadership is contextualized through a masculine lens, and feminine-coded traits are undervalued, women in positions of authority often face a no-win situation. This is known as the double-bind: if a woman displays stereotypically feminine traits (such as empathy, cooperation, and emotional intelligence), she may be seen as likeable, but not as a leader. If she adopts more masculine-coded traits (such as assertiveness, decisiveness, or authoritativeness), she may be viewed as competent, but also as cold, aggressive, or unlikable. Women cannot win.

One influential framework, known as role congruity theory, explains this tension as a conflict between gender norms and leadership norms.[11] Women are expected to be warm and communal, but leaders are expected to be assertive and dominant. Conforming to one expectation means violating the other. This tension is especially pronounced in male-dominated fields like law, in which traits such as assertiveness, stamina, and authoritativeness are often seen as markers of credibility and leadership potential. As a result, women who aspire to senior roles may feel they must constantly calibrate their behavior; being tough, but not too tough; confident, but not arrogant; warm, but not soft. Over time, this pressure to walk a behavioral tightrope can lead to exhaustion, self-doubt, and imposter syndrome – not because of any personal failing, but because the system itself is built on conflicting expectations.

Further research supports this pattern. The double-bind does not just mean being judged differently; it actually means being penalized either way. A 2007 report found that women leaders are often criticized both for showing too little or too much assertiveness. One research participant summarized it in this way: "Women are caught in a Catch-22 situation regarding leadership. If they are strong they are seen to be aggressive, and if they work more in a consultative way they are seen to be weak".[12] The very traits seen as strengths in men are reframed as flaws in women.

This echoed my own experience. As I shared earlier, when I secured a significant client win through persistence and independent effort, I was told I had not "credited others enough". Rather than being recognized for my initiative, I was perceived as too independent in a team in which, ironically, the male partners routinely worked alone and guarded opportunities. I had delivered an outstanding result, but the way I had done it did not fit the mold of how women were expected to behave.

Transactional v transformational leadership

What would happen if we stopped asking women to change, and instead re-examined what good leadership actually looks like? That is the question psychologist Alice Eagly set out to explore in her influential research on leadership styles. In a landmark 2003 meta-analysis, Eagly and her colleagues analyzed data from 45 studies comparing the behaviors of male and female leaders across a range of organizational settings.[13] They found a consistent pattern: men were more likely to use a "transactional" or "laissez-faire" style, while women were more likely to adopt a "transformational" approach.

Transactional leadership is typically characterized by:

- Exchanging rewards for performance;
- Monitoring for mistakes or rule-breaking; and
- Applying correction or punishment when expectations are not met.

This model aligns closely with hierarchical workplace cultures, in which authority is maintained through control, compliance, and performance metrics. It is often associated with masculine-coded traits, such as assertiveness, dominance, and rationality.

Transformational leadership, by contrast, focuses on:

- Idealized influence (leading by example);
- Inspirational motivation (articulating a shared, compelling vision);
- Intellectual stimulation (encouraging innovation and creative thinking); and
- Individualized consideration (coaching and developing others).[14]

Eagly's findings matter, because transformational leadership – the style more frequently associated with women – has been shown to be more effective in driving team engagement, performance, and long-term success. Many of its key qualities overlap with feminine-coded traits: empathy, adaptability, collaboration, and emotional intelligence. However, because these traits are not typically celebrated in law firm cultures, they are often undervalued in performance reviews, overlooked in partnership decisions, and absent from traditional ideas of "executive presence". Eagly and her co-authors note that transformational behaviors – particularly individual consideration and inspirational motivation – can be especially effective forms of women's leadership, but organizational cultures often fail to recognize or reward them. Their research reframes the conversation. The problem is not that women do not fit the leadership mold – it's that the mold itself may be too narrow... or the wrong shape altogether.

Later in this chapter, I share insights from my interviews with senior female legal leaders who are proving what is possible. They are demonstrating highly effective transformational leadership: motivating through vision, fostering growth, and building trust. They lead with clarity, compassion, and strategic acumen, and their firms aren't just functioning – they're thriving. Their stories offer compelling evidence that redefining leadership is not a compromise; it is a competitive advantage.

The consequences: how gendered leadership norms play out in law firms

The research shows that leadership is still culturally coded as male, and that women face a double-bind when they do not conform. However, the real impact of these dynamics is felt in the everyday stories shared by women lawyers themselves. In Female Lawyers' Club and beyond, women have repeatedly described how they have been penalized for demonstrating the very traits that leadership frameworks celebrate in men: assertiveness, confidence, ambition, and independence. These are the traits that form part of partnership criteria; however, when embodied by women, they can trigger discomfort, criticism, and career-limiting consequences.

When I asked women in Female Lawyers' Club and on LinkedIn, "Have you ever been penalized for being assertive, direct, ambitious, independent, or confident – traits often praised in men but questioned in women?", the responses were overwhelming. What emerged wasn't just frustration, but a powerful chorus of collective discrimination:

> *"I was told as a junior associate I was too 'chippy'. And that was by a woman."*

> *"In one of my first one-to-ones at a well-known firm, my (female) manager told me I wasn't 'very approachable.' Why? Because I wasn't smiley enough, and my emails were 'too formal.'"*

> *"I've been told to 'pipe down' before."*

> *"I was called 'aggressive' this afternoon by a male counterpart for simply responding to blunt emails with the same energy."*

> *"I smashed my billable target and was told I was too junior for a bonus. I'd done everything right – and still got nothing."*

> *"They said I had 'sharp elbows', but all I did was set high standards and get things done."*

These are not minor criticisms, but reflect a deeper discomfort with women taking up space, owning their voices, or claiming success. Leadership traits, when expressed by women, are often rebranded as flaws. One lawyer described posting about positive client feedback on LinkedIn, only to be chastised by management for "making others feel bad":

> *"The post was anonymous and professional. But it became clear that ambition and visibility were being policed, not praised."*

Another described being labeled "an alpha female" and accused of having "too much testosterone" by male colleagues. Her ambition was seen as threatening, rather than admirable. When she left a senior City role for a new partner position at a regional firm, her former boss (a woman) told others she was "taking a career break due to separation anxiety from her 1-year-old". The assumption that motherhood had curtailed her ambition was not just untrue – it was a projection rooted in stereotype. It is not only women's ambition that is policed – their empathy can be, too. The legal profession has long equated professionalism with detachment, rewarding those who maintain distance and control, rather than those who lead with care. One barrister described the pressure to suppress her humanity in order to fit in:

> *"During my 6 years in a London set of Chambers, often working on harrowing criminal cases, I was frequently told that I should care less about my clients, develop a thick skin, put on a hard shell, and just 'get on with the job'. Neither my peers, judges, nor the majority of my colleagues seemed to value in the slightest my heightened sense of humanity – the genuine concern and gentle hand on the shoulder of a terrified, pregnant young woman just sentenced to a term of imprisonment; the begging of court staff for a few more minutes to provide some comfort and reassurance to a distressed client detained in the cells; a whispered word to prison staff to request that a vulnerable person be placed on suicide watch; missing a train home to talk through the options with anxious family members. Whilst I was not the only person to show such care to her clients, I was in a small minority, and regularly saw colleagues leaving a distraught client with a perfunctory 'all the best' and pat on the back, before heading off to the robing room for a good laugh and chinwag about the latest football results."*

These pressures are not just cultural – they have material consequences. The ways in which women are judged for their behavior can significantly affect their progression and the outcome of their careers. Women I spoke to recounted being passed over for promotion despite meeting all the criteria, only to watch male colleagues promoted under more flexible timelines; being told that they were "too confident" when they articulated achievements; and then criticized for being invisible when they toned it down. One lawyer put it as such:

"The way women acknowledge others and say it was a team effort, or use 'we' instead of 'I', means they're often overlooked for their personal achievements. [However], if we self-promote, we're told we're too much."

This is the double-bind in action, exacerbated by internal processes that reward dominant behaviors (like speaking up first in meetings or competing for client credit), often without questioning whether those behaviors truly reflect leadership capability. One lawyer shared the way in which her ambition and assertiveness had been judged negatively by colleagues and, surprisingly, more often by other women than by men:

"I've had more judgment from other female colleagues than male ones, and the more vindictive behavior has come from women. I'm very forthright and outspoken; in the dominating world of law, that seems to trigger some people. I believe in supporting others and bringing people up behind me. But that hasn't always been welcomed."

This observation reflects a painful truth: gendered expectations are often reinforced horizontally, not just from above. When the system demands conformity, it can be women themselves who feel pressured to uphold those rules, perhaps out of fear, survival, or internalized bias. Another lawyer told me:

"I was dealing with a difficult client who refused to listen to me but immediately accepted the same advice when it came from a male colleague. He wouldn't even refer to me by name. Just 'the lawyer'."

Others shared similar experiences:

"Male peers who pushed back on workloads were praised for setting boundaries. I was told I was the problem, and that my work would now be monitored."

One woman shared a series of experiences that illustrate how bias plays out across multiple stages of career progression:

"I was described as 'aggressive' by my head of department simply for standing my ground. I didn't raise my voice – I was just matter of fact. But it was still labelled aggression."

The consequences went beyond perception; they affected her career. During succession planning, she wasn't invited to apply for the head of department role. At the time, she was pregnant and working 4 days a week. Full-time, in-office expectations were quietly written into the job description, which she could not meet:

> *"It was all set up so I couldn't do it. I didn't even get a reply to my email declining to apply because it wasn't feasible. After my maternity leave, I was offered a choice: return to an office that didn't work for my setup, or take redundancy."*

These are not isolated incidents. They are patterns, baked into systems of evaluation, feedback, and progression, and they come at a cost: to women's confidence, wellbeing, and long-term retention in the profession. The real power of these stories lies in their truth: they remind us that gender bias isn't theoretical; it's woven into the lived experience of talented women across the legal profession. If we want to change the culture of leadership, we must start by truly listening.

The shift: a new model of leadership

While the legal profession has long held onto a narrow idea of leadership, often favoring traits such as assertiveness, control, and individual dominance, there are clear signs that a broader, more inclusive model is gaining traction. A growing body of research suggests that leadership grounded in emotional intelligence, collaboration, and adaptability is not only more inclusive; it's also more effective. A 2020 *Harvard Business Review* analysis of 360-degree feedback data found that women outperformed men in 17 out of 19 key leadership competencies, including taking initiative, acting with resilience, displaying high integrity, and inspiring and motivating others.[15] These should not be dismissed as "soft" skills; they are the skills that drive high performance, especially in complex, people-driven environments like law.

Meanwhile, large-scale studies by Deloitte and the World Economic Forum have pointed to a global shift toward more human-centered leadership.[16, 17] This research identifies inclusive leadership – a management style that values diversity, ensures all voices are heard, and actively creates a sense of belonging – as a core driver of innovation, psychological safety, and long-term business resilience. These are qualities increasingly valued by both clients and talent.

This shift is not only being led from the top, but is also driven by a new generation of professionals with different expectations of leadership and workplace culture. In EY's 2022 US Generation Survey, 39 percent of Gen Z and millennials said that company culture has "a great deal" of influence on whether they would stay with an employer, compared to 29 percent of Baby Boomers; indeed, 76 percent of millennials said they'd go so far as to leave a job if DEI initiatives were not offered.[18] In a profession in which talent retention is an increasing challenge, this change in expectations cannot be ignored.

These shifts are not just generational; they are global. In *The Athena Doctrine*, John Gerzema and Michael D'Antonio surveyed over 64,000 people across 13 countries and found that qualities traditionally seen as "feminine", such as empathy, honesty, collaboration, and flexibility, were increasingly viewed as essential to effective leadership, business success, and societal progress.[19] The authors asked participants to rank 125 leadership traits and, across cultures, the most highly valued qualities aligned with those historically coded as feminine. Respondents expressed frustration with traditional, hierarchical, command-and-control leadership models, particularly in the wake of financial and political crises. One striking finding was that 66 percent of participants, including both men and women, agreed that the world would be a better place if men thought more like women.[20] This was not about reversing gender roles; it was about embracing a broader, more emotionally intelligent and human-centered approach to leadership. The study revealed a widespread appetite for change: a move away from rigid, individualistic models of power toward a more inclusive, collaborative, and value-driven leadership style – one that reflects the complexity of the world we live in, and the kind of leadership people increasingly want to follow.

It is important to be clear: this is not about feminizing leadership; it is about broadening it. Inclusive leadership does not mean rejecting traditionally valued qualities, like decisiveness or confidence. Instead, it means expanding the toolkit to include a wider, more balanced range of capabilities, and a recognition that empathy, adaptability, humility, and emotional intelligence are not "extras" or "nice-to-haves". They are core competencies and, increasingly, competitive advantages.

The challenge for the legal profession now is not to decide whether these traits matter (they clearly do), but whether the systems we have built – from promotion frameworks to cultural norms – are designed to recognize and reward them.

Redefining leadership on our own terms

The traditional view of legal leadership has long been synonymous with control, competitiveness, and rationality over emotion. However, for many women in law, and a growing number of their colleagues across all genders, these traits no longer represent the leadership they admire or aspire to. As part of my research for this chapter, I had the pleasure of interviewing various senior women leaders. In talking to these inspirational women, a different picture of leadership emerged: one rooted in empathy, integrity, courage, and care.

Christine Braamskamp, managing partner at Jenner & Block London LLP, described leadership not as power over others, but as "listening first, not reacting too fast, and encouraging everyone to speak up, no matter who they are". In her words, good leadership means having "the confidence to say when something doesn't feel right, and the courage to do the right thing even when it's hard". This more human-centered approach isn't just more inclusive; it is more effective. The ability to tune into what is really going on in a room; to make people feel seen; and to respond with clarity and emotional intelligence is what builds trust. It also gets results.

I once saw this play out during a particularly memorable pitch. A male colleague and I were bidding to deliver training for the entire workforce of a major UK organization. We delivered our presentation. During the final Q&A session, I noticed that the lead decision-maker looked slightly uneasy. It wasn't anything she said, but a shift in her tone, a slight hesitation in her body language. I sensed that she was not sure that we truly understood the significance of what they were trusting us with. So, I spoke directly to it: I told her we saw this work as an honor; that it mattered to us; and that we would treat it with the high degree of care it deserved. Afterwards, on the way back from the presentation, my colleague told me: "You won us that tender." He had not picked up on the hesitation, and he acknowledged that my ability to sense and address it had made all the difference. The contract was worth £100,000 and was won not with legal acumen, but with emotional intelligence – one of the most underrated of leadership strengths.

Alison Eddy, former London managing partner and current partner ambassador for inclusion at Irwin Mitchell LLP, reflected candidly on the shift in ideal leadership:

> *"When I started out, there was a tendency to emulate the men, to fit in. But, actually, being able to bring your whole self, being able to show compassion and vulnerability – that's what really builds trust and loyalty."*

This reflects what author and academic Brené Brown calls "daring leadership": the ability to lead with vulnerability, courage, and clarity, rather than defensiveness, control, or perfectionism. In *Dare to Lead*, Brown writes: "Clear is kind. Unclear is unkind."[21] This philosophy resonates deeply with the women I spoke to, who emphasized clarity, honesty, and consistency as the cornerstones of their leadership. Rachael Heenan, senior partner at Capsticks LLP, spoke to me about the power of building genuine relationships:

> *"Leadership isn't about shouting the loudest. It's about taking the time to understand your people: their pressures, their strengths, their lives outside work, and making them feel valued."*

This emphasis on understanding and connection is echoed by others in senior leadership. It reflects a growing recognition that authenticity and empathy are not at odds with authority; they are, in fact, integral to it. Sara Bailey, senior partner at Trowers & Hamlins LLP, puts it succinctly:

> *"To be a truly great leader, you need to be authentic. You can be authentic and still have gravitas. You need to lead from the front, be relatable, and embody the values of your organization."*

Another powerful example of value-led leadership comes from Jo Farmer, who used her appointment as joint managing partner at Lewis Silkin LLP as an opportunity to challenge language and structures that reinforced hierarchy and separation. She explains:

> *"When I was elected to the managing partner role, I looked at some of the structures, including the use of 'divisions' within the firm ... And one of the first things I did was to move away from 'divisions' into more of a holistic structure of clusters and groups to make people think more as one firm. Even the word 'division' is divisive!"*

This seemingly small change reflects a deeper commitment to unity and inclusivity through an intentional move away from siloed thinking and towards a collaborative culture. By questioning long-standing terminology, Farmer demonstrates the way in which leadership can shape culture through clarity of language and a clear vision for belonging. Farmer also reimagined the balance between leadership and fee-earning, consciously stepping away from the traditional expectations of leaders juggling full client workloads. She shares:

> *"For decades, it's been pretty common to have managing partners that try to manage alongside a full fee-earning role, which is pretty unbelievable considering the demands of the job ... In law firms, I think that one of the reasons for this is that, traditionally, the men in the role have been apprehensive about giving up their identity in their fee-earning. They're also scared about the 'what ifs' ... I've almost given up my fee-earning role, (although I still make sure I see clients regularly to understand what they are saying and what they need). I'm now fully devoted to understanding the partners, the future of the business, the clients and the strategy ... The results we're now having wouldn't have happened unless I'd had the time to sit with people and coach them through changes."*

By making space to focus on people, business development, and strategy, Farmer demonstrates how letting go of legacy leadership expectations can create greater impact. Her example challenges the long-held belief that fee-earning work is the only mark of value and invites a broader view of what great leadership can look like in law firms.

Across all the conversations I had, a common theme emerged: good leadership is human leadership. It is about enabling others to thrive, not simply asserting your authority, and creating a culture of safety and trust, in which people feel able to contribute, grow, and even challenge you. Importantly, each of these leaders demonstrated that this approach does not mean compromising on results. Their firms are high-performing and commercially successful. What their stories show is that inclusive, emotionally intelligent leadership is not a nice-to-have; it is a competitive advantage. This is the model of leadership that is already delivering results, and it is about time we adopted it more widely across the profession.

What needs to change: shifting cultures, systems, and self-perception

Redefining leadership in law is not just a mindset shift; it is a structural and cultural matter. To move beyond outdated models and create space for truly inclusive leadership, we need change at every level: systemic, cultural, and personal.

The systemic shift: what firms need to rethink

Progress will not be possible if leadership potential continues to be measured using outdated metrics. Many of the systems in law firms today – from promotion pathways to client origination models – were designed in another era that promoted different assumptions about who gets to lead and why. If we want more diverse and sustainable leadership, we need to update these systems to reflect what we now know drives performance, retention, and trust.

Promotion frameworks are a key starting point. Too often, the criteria for advancement reward visibility over value, favoring those who speak the loudest, occupy the most space, or conform to traditional models of authority. Traits like dominance, control, and self-promotion are still implicitly recognized as leadership behaviors. However, as we have seen, research and real-world outcomes show that these are not the only – or even the most effective – predictors of leadership success. Firms could instead adopt more holistic promotion criteria that capture a wider range of leadership behaviors. 360-degree feedback models are one example, as these gather insights from not just supervisors, but also from peers, direct reports, and clients. This provides a broader and more accurate picture of a leader's true impact. It also allows for leadership traits such as mentoring, collaboration, and emotional intelligence to be recognized as integral, rather than peripheral, to firm success. Rachael Heenan noted something similar about successful leadership in her interview:

> *"The most effective leaders I've worked with are the ones who invest in people: who create the conditions for others to thrive, not just themselves. That impact doesn't always show up on traditional metrics, but it absolutely matters."*

Some firms have already started evolving their frameworks. At Clifford Chance, inclusive leadership is a central pillar of its global talent strategy. The firm has introduced initiatives such as reverse mentoring, employee networks, and inclusion training to help ensure leadership opportunities are accessible and equitable across the organization.[22, 23]

Another area that needs reform is client origination and credit. Origination systems tend to reward those who are already well-networked or in positions of power, which is most often men. This can create a cycle in which influence accumulates in the hands of a few, and those working hard behind the scenes (often women) remain invisible when credit is allocated. To break this cycle, some firms are now experimenting with shared credit models, in which success is attributed more broadly to the team involved, recognizing not only who brought the client in but also who grew and retained the relationship. A more equitable credit system would acknowledge that client work is often collaborative, and that sustaining relationships over time is as valuable as opening the door. Christine Braamskamp commented:

> *"Too often, success is still individualised. But we know in practice that client work is collaborative, and we should reward it that way."*

Some firms are beginning to rethink how they reward collaboration. US firm Mintz, for example, recently revised its compensation model to encourage greater sharing of origination credit, capping the originating partner's credit at 75 percent on large matters and promoting more team-based recognition. Research from Harvard Law School's Center on the Legal Profession reinforces this view, suggesting that partners who actively involve colleagues in client work –rather than guarding relationships – consistently grow larger books of business.[24] In other words, collaboration is not just fairer; it also makes strategic sense. These models not only reward long-term client care, but dismantle the myth of the lone rainmaker. However, evolving frameworks and credit models are only part of the solution. If firms are serious about developing more inclusive leaders, they must also invest in training and support as standard, not as a nice-to-have. Sara Bailey put it in this way:

> *"We need to be much better at providing proper support and training for those in management. It's still regarded as a favour to give someone access to a coach – but it should be seen as essential."*

Bailey is right: too often, we expect people to lead instinctively, without giving them the tools to succeed. Leadership development should be proactive, not remedial.

Finally, we must rethink leadership pipelines. It is not enough to recruit diverse talent at the junior level and hope it rises to the top. The pipeline itself needs scaffolding: transparent development programs; clearly defined leadership pathways; and active sponsorship, not just mentorship, for those underrepresented at the top. Alison Eddy reflected:

> *"I didn't have a sponsor early in my career, and I know now how much difference that would have made. You need someone in the room speaking for you, not just advising you outside it."*

There is growing recognition within the legal profession that traditional leadership pipelines may overlook key interpersonal strengths. As reported in *PD Quarterly*, law firms "are beginning to catch up with their clients in the use of assessments to improve how they hire, develop, and promote their talent".[25] These conversations suggest an opening for tools like the Emotional Quotient Inventory (EQi 2.0) or the Myers–Briggs Type Indicator (MBTI) to support structured identification and growth of leadership potential. These tools can help to identify lawyers with the kinds of interpersonal skills that clients increasingly value – empathy, adaptability, humility, and relationship-building – and ensure that those strengths are supported as part of leadership development.

Without these changes, we risk continuing to ask women and others from underrepresented backgrounds to adapt themselves to systems that were never designed with them in mind. In doing so, we miss out on the kind of leadership that could genuinely transform our profession for the better.

The cultural shift: expanding the leadership imagination

Alongside systems, we must challenge deeply held cultural assumptions, including the idea that there is only one "right" way to lead. Leadership does not need to be loud to be strong or dominate to drive results. Rachael Heenan put it like this:

> *"We need to stop pretending that leadership is one-size-fits-all. Some of the best leaders I've worked with were collaborative, not commanding. They created space for others to thrive. That's what real leadership looks like."*

Cultural change happens when those in power model new behaviors, validate different leadership styles, and champion inclusive traits as part of firm identity, not as exceptions or add-ons. At Jenner & Block, Christine Braamskamp is doing just that:

> *"I am very conscious about how I show up. I try to lead by actively modelling the behaviours I expect of others: showing respect for other people's perspectives and opinions; being client-focused; putting the firm first;*

> *getting stuck into the last-minute work demands alongside the team; taking time for my family and talking about it; [and] valuing every member of the office and acknowledging that everyone has a role to play in the success of the endeavour. I think, when you do that consistently, people trust you; they feel safe, and they perform better."*

Jo Farmer has discovered that showing up as herself resonates widely. She began sharing her story openly and found that authenticity builds trust:

> *"I'm experimenting a bit on LinkedIn, being quite public about my journey and the fact that I've come from a less privileged background and some of the issues I find as a female managing partner. I had an inkling that it needed to be said, and the reaction has persuaded me that it absolutely needed to be said. People are just saying, 'Thank God somebody is actually showing a little bit more of a human approach to things.'"*

Her experience echoes Brené Brown's research on the power of vulnerability. Brown's work demonstrates that, when leaders are willing to be open about their challenges and imperfections, it builds connection, trust, and psychological safety in teams, which are key ingredients in resilient, high-performing organizations.[26]

Beyond that, several firms stand out for embedding inclusion into culture:

- Irwin Mitchell have exceeded gender parity in their partnership by embedding inclusion into performance metrics: Alison Eddy explains: "At Irwin Mitchell ... 58 percent of partners are women. It's largely because management bought in; diversity objectives are written into standard performance conversations ... Culture is a critical business asset."
- Seyfarth Shaw delivers Inclusive Leadership training firm-wide, to equip leaders with the skills and accountability needed to model inclusive behavior. They have also promoted a more diverse leadership: their executive committee includes women, Latina, Black, and LGBTQ+ partners.[27]
- Finnegan, a global IP firm, applies the Mansfield Rule, ensuring that at least 30 percent of candidates for leadership roles are women, minorities, or LGBTQ+ lawyers.[28]
- Reed Smith won an award for gender equality by creating an environment in which women have equal opportunity to succeed. Since the

pandemic, the firm has introduced several female-focused initiatives, including The Family Network, to help balance work and personal responsibilities, and the Women's Initiative Network of Reed Smith, which offers development support, mentoring, and training. The firm was also a founding member of the Reignite Academy, which supports lawyers returning to practice after a career break. In 2023, 50 percent of newly promoted partners were women, with women now representing 26 percent of the firm's equity partnership.[29]
- Morgan Lewis has earned the "Mansfield Certification Plus" multiple years running, an award that recognizes firms actively curating a pipeline of diverse leadership.

These actions demonstrate a shift from passive DEI statements to active, measured cultural practice. These firms are not treating inclusive behaviors as optional; they are core to how leadership operates. Lewis Silkin's approach demonstrates what these values look like in practice. Jo Farmer explains:

> *"This idea of working yourself to the bone – being present at all times and being on the precipice of being burnt out – has got to go. At Lewis Silkin, we're really clear that we don't want people to be burnt out and we want them to have meaningful leave. We track anyone who's done over 200 hours in a month and talk to their manager about how long the project will go on. At the end of the project, they get additional time off – a week, 2 weeks, even a minisabbatical – because you need meaningful time off to decompress after those big projects."*

The firm's retention rates and market performance demonstrate that a humane culture is not just good ethics; it is good business.

The personal shift: leading without shrinking or shapeshifting

Finally, there is the inner shift, which might be the most transformative of all. For many women in law, the challenge is not just being overlooked; it is the constant pressure to shrink, self-censor, or shapeshift to fit a narrow ideal. Many women must act like someone else just to be taken seriously. Let's be clear: this is not just exhausting, but wasteful. Every moment spent second-guessing yourself, masking your instincts, or editing your personality is energy that could be channeled into being the most powerful version of yourself that can most effectively lead others. As *Dare to Lead* author Brené

Brown writes, authenticity is not a feel-good extra; it's a leadership imperative. It enables courage, builds trust, and acts as the foundation for lasting impact.

Author Daniel Goleman's research on emotional intelligence demonstrates that the most effective leaders excel in five key areas:

- Self-awareness: Knowing your strengths, weaknesses, and emotional triggers;
- Self-regulation: Staying calm under pressure and managing your impulses;
- Motivation: Having a strong internal drive to achieve beyond expectations;
- Empathy: Understanding others' emotions and perspectives; and
- Social skills: Building strong relationships and managing conflict effectively.[30]

These are essential elements that enable leaders to build trust, inspire performance, and navigate complexity. When we give ourselves permission to lead with empathy, emotional awareness, and genuine connection, we draw on strengths that are more enduring and impactful than dominance or control. For a long time, I thought I had to tone parts of myself down to be seen as credible. That meant suppressing the parts of me that felt too human — my empathy, warmth, and instinct. I felt under pressure to present as a corporate clone: all logic, no emotion. However, that wasn't me. When I started showing up more authentically, especially in places that valued contribution over conformity, everything began to change. Over time, I started to notice that the traits I had been most unsure about were the ones that made me stand out and helped me to succeed. Clients valued the fact that I listened and understood where they were coming from, and colleagues trusted me because I was straightforward. The work I won wasn't due to bravado – it came from being thoughtful, human, and honest.

What would happen if you stopped editing yourself? What if you leaned into the parts of you that make people feel safe, inspired, or seen? We do not need to fit the mold; we need to break it and build something better in its place. Rachael Heenan reinforces this:

> *"I realised early on that I wasn't going to lead like the men who came before me, and that was okay. Because, when I showed up as myself, people responded. That's when the real impact started to happen."*

So, what can you do, right now?

- Take stock of the qualities you've felt pressure to tone down in the past, such as empathy, enthusiasm, intuition, or vulnerability. What if those were not flaws to fix, but strengths to harness? If you are not sure what your strengths are, take a look at the box below.
- Notice when you're self-editing and ask yourself: what am I afraid might happen if I fully showed up as myself? Who might feel more inspired, empowered, or safe if I did?
- Reflect on when and where you feel most authentic to yourself and how you might bring more of that version of you to work.
- Surround yourself with people and mentors who value the real you, not a copy of someone else.

Discovering your unique leadership strengths

If you're not sure what your strengths are, take a moment to reflect on the following:

- When have you felt most energized, proud, or effective at work? What qualities were you using in those moments: empathy, clarity, or creativity?
- What do others consistently appreciate about you? Ask several trusted colleagues or friends: "What's something I do really well that you value?"
- What comes naturally to you? These are the things that you do effortlessly, like bringing calm to a crisis or helping others feel heard. They may be your greatest assets.

Your strengths do not need to look like anyone else's. Often, the traits you have felt pressure to minimize are exactly what your clients, team, and the profession need more of.

Redefining leadership starts with reclaiming your own style. This is not about waiting for permission; it is about showing up, fully and unapologetically, and recognizing that many of the traits so often excluded from the traditional leadership playbook are not flaws – they are strengths. It is time we led like it.

The opportunity: redefining leadership; reclaiming ourselves

Leadership in law doesn't need to be reimagined from scratch; rather, it needs to be reclaimed. Throughout this chapter, we have seen the ways in which the traditional leadership model has been built on narrow foundations: rewarding visibility over value; dominance over empathy; and individual gain over collective success. These models have long shaped how leadership is defined, who gets to be seen as a leader, and who is asked to adapt themselves to fit these requirements.

However, those foundations are shifting. The stories of the senior women leaders we have heard from, and the research discussed in this chapter, show that a different kind of leadership is not only possible, but already existent and functional. This is a leadership style rooted in clarity, courage, emotional intelligence, and care – one that values results, but not at the cost of authenticity or inclusion. The opportunity open to us now is not just to create space for women to lead, but to change what leadership means in the first place. That means:

- For firms and their cultures: Rethinking how leadership is identified, measured, and rewarded, and dismantling systems that exclude by default. It means validating a wider range of leadership styles as legitimate and effective, not peripheral or exceptional. Inclusion should not be an initiative on the sidelines; it should be embedded into the very fabric of what success looks like.
- For individuals: Unlearning the belief that we need to change who we are to succeed and reclaiming the full range of our leadership strengths.

This change will not happen by accident; it requires deliberate, sustained action. It needs voices like yours calling for change from the inside and people who are willing to show up differently, lead differently, and back others who do the same. So, whether you are a junior associate or a managing partner, a general counsel, or a lawyer returning after a break, here is the call: don't wait to be invited. Start leading as yourself, not an edited or overly polished version. Instead, be the version of you that listens more than she talks and who leads with care, asks brave questions, and builds others up instead of crowding them out. That is not soft leadership; that is future-proof leadership. Christine Braamskamp recommends:

> *"Clients – especially sophisticated ones – are looking for emotionally intelligent advisers who can lead with integrity."*

Jo Farmer's advice to the next generation is simple but powerful:

> *"Be yourself and model something different, because the industry is ready for it. There's a talent war out there so, if you're at a firm where you're well-paid but uninspired by the style of leadership, there are other firms modelling a different approach. You shouldn't have to settle for something that doesn't feel authentically you. Be brave, and absolutely don't settle for second best."*

Sara Bailey echoes this sentiment, emphasizing both authenticity and a growth mindset as essential for the leaders of tomorrow:

> *"Be yourself. Be honest about your strengths and weaknesses and build a team around you that complement you. The most important piece of advice I'd give is to keep learning. You never stop being open to change."*

This is not about perfection, but about honesty, adaptability, and the courage to lead from who you are, not who the system told you to be. The world is changing fast, and the legal profession must change with it. We can no longer afford to leave talent untapped, voices unheard, or leadership potential unrecognized, simply because it does not fit into a dated ideal.

The next generation is watching, as are clients. However, perhaps most importantly, so are the women coming up behind us, hoping someone will show them that there is more than one way to lead, and that who they are is not a liability, but an asset. Let us be that someone and show them – and ourselves – what is possible.

References

1 Solicitors Regulation Authority, "Diversity in law firms' workforce", 3 January 2025. See: https://www.sra.org.uk/sra/equality-diversity/diversity-profession/diverse-legal-profession

2 National Association for Law Placement, 2023 *Report on Diversity in U.S. Law Firms*, January 2024. See: https://www.nalp.org/uploads/Research/2023NALPReportonDiversityFinal.pdf

3 The National Jurist, "Women represent 55 percent of associate positions at U.S. law firms, NALP reports", 3 February 2025. See: https://nationaljurist.com/national-jurist/news/women-represent-55-of-associate-positions-at-u-s-law-firms-nalp-reports

4 Learn R. and Violante D., *Overview of Gender Diversity in Business Law: A Research Compendium*, October 2022. See: https://www.law.berkeley.edu/wp-content/uploads/2022/10/Overview-of-Gender-Diversity-in-Business-Law-1.pdf

5 Slaughter and May, *UK Pay Gap Report 2024*, 2025. See: https://www.slaughterandmay.com/media/mm4l2qfv/uk-pay-gap-report-2024.pdf

6 Ashurst, *UK Pay Gap Report 2024*, April 2025. See: https://www.ashurst.com/-/media/Ashurst/Documents/SXA-documents/Pay-Gap-Reports/UK-Pay-Gap-Report-2024-FINAL.pdf

7 Schein V.E., "The relationship between sex role stereotypes and requisite management characteristics", J *Appl Psychol*, 1973, volume 57, issue 2, pp. 95–100. doi: 10.1037/h0037128

8 Schein V. E., "A global look at psychological barriers to women's progress in management", *Journal of Social Issues*, 2001, volume 57, issue 4, pp. 675–688. https://doi.org/10.1111/0022-4537.00235

9 Eagly A. H. and Johnson B. T., "Gender and leadership style: A meta-analysis", *Psychological Bulletin*, 1990, volume 108, issue 2, pp. 233–256. https://doi.org/10.1037/0033-2909.108.2.233

10 Eagly A.H. and Johannesen-Schmidt M.C., "The Leadership Styles of Women and Men", *Journal of Social Issues*, 2001, issue 57, pp. 781–797. https://doi.org/10.1111/0022-4537.00241

11 Eagly A.H. and Karau S.J., "Role Congruity Theory of Prejudice Toward Female Leaders", *Psychological Review*, 2002, volume 109, issue 3. https://doi.org/10.1037/0033-295X.109.3.573

12 Catalyst, "The double-bind dilemma for women in leadership: Damned if you do, doomed if you don't", 15 July 2007. See: https://www.catalyst.org/research/the-double-bind-dilemma-for-women-in-leadership-damned-if-you-do-doomed-if-you-dont/

13 Eagly A.H., Johannesen-Schmidt M.C., and van Engen M.L., "Transformational, transactional, and laissez-faire leadership styles: A meta-analysis comparing women and men", *Psychological Bulletin*, 2003, volume 129, issue 4, pp. 569–591. https://doi.org/10.1037/0033-2909.129.4.569

14 Bass B.M. and Avolio B.J., *Improving Organizational Effectiveness Through Transformational Leadership*, Thousand Oaks (CA): Sage; 1994

15 Zenger J. and Folkman J., "Research: Women Are Better Leaders During a Crisis", *Harvard Business Review*, 30 December 2020. See: https://hbr.org/2020/12/research-women-are-better-leaders-during-a-crisis

16 World Economic Forum, *Global Gender Gap Report 2023*, 20 June 2023. See: https://www.weforum.org/reports/global-gender-gap-report-2023

17 Van Durme Y., Commisso C., Flynn J., Griffiths M., and Guziak J., "Evolving leadership to drive human performance", Deloitte, 5 February 2024. See: https://www.deloitte.com/us/en/insights/topics/talent/human-capital-trends/2024/human-performance-new-ways-of-working.html

18 EY, *2022 EY US Generation Survey*, 13 October 2022. See: https://www.ey.com/content/dam/ey-unified-site/ey-com/en-us/campaigns/diversity-equity-inclusiveness/documents/ey-generational-exec-summary.pdf

19 Gerzema J. and D'Antonio M., *The Athena Doctrine: How Women (and the Men Who Think Like Them) Will Rule the Future*, San Francisco (CA): Jossey-Bass; 2013
20 *Ibid.*
21 Brown B., *Dare to Lead: Brave Work. Tough Conversations. Whole Hearts*, New York (NY): Random House; 2018
22 Clifford Chance, *Responsible Business Report 2023: Future Focus*, 2023. See: https://www.cliffordchance.com/content/dam/cliffordchance/About_us/responsible-business/2023/2023-responsible-business-report.pdf
23 Clifford Chance, "Our inclusive culture", 2025. See: https://jobs.cliffordchance.com/our-culture-uk
24 Gardner H.K., "Collaboration in Law Firms", *The Practice*, September/October 2015. https://clp.law.harvard.edu/article/collaboration-in-law-firms
25 Forrest B., "Catching Up with Our Clients: Using Assessments to Manage Our Talent More Effectively", *PD Quarterly*, February 2015, pp. 5–21. https://firmleader.com/media/Using-Assessments-to-Manage-Our-Talent-More-Effectively.pdf
26 Brown B., *Dare to Lead: Brave Work. Tough Conversations. Whole Hearts*, New York (NY): Random House; 2018
27 Kapolitz K., "Best Law Firms for Women & Diversity: The DEI Best Practices Behind the Numbers", Seramount, 1 June 2023. See: https://seramount.com/articles/best-law-firms-for-women-diversity-the-dei-best-practices-behind-the-numbers/
28 *Ibid.*
29 Edwards B., "Who won Women and Diversity in Law Awards – and why – Diversity, Equity and Inclusion categories", *Global Legal Post*, 22 March 2023. See: https://www.globallegalpost.com/news/who-won-women-and-diversity-in-law-awards-and-why-diversity-equity-and-inclusion-categories-1101937316?
30 Goleman D., "What Makes a Leader?", *Harvard Business Review*, 2004. See: https://hbr.org/2004/01/what-makes-a-leader

Chapter 3: Technology, gender, and justice: AI's role in women's advancement in the legal profession

By Priya Lele, chair and cofounder of She Breaks the Law, and Shilpa Bhandarkar, legal innovation and AI consultant

It is undeniable that artificial intelligence (AI), particularly this new wave of generative AI (genAI), is having a transformational impact on the legal industry. It is an incredibly exciting time to be a lawyer and to have access to new and innovative tools that can streamline research, accelerate contract review, and reimagine the ways in which legal advice is delivered. However, multiple studies have highlighted an emerging and concerning gender gap in the adoption of this technology. A collaborative paper by researchers from Berkeley, Harvard, and Stanford found that the gender gap in genAI usage persisted across nearly all regions, sectors, and occupations, with the authors noting that "the gender gap in adoption is nearly universal ... from mothers in Mumbai to managers in Madrid, women use AI less than men".[1]

Recent research by Deloitte has reinforced this finding, highlighting a gender gap in genAI adoption across multiple geographies. Women's adoption of genAI in the US was roughly a third lower than that of men: 33 percent of women reported experimenting with genAI or using it for projects and tasks beyond experimentation, compared with 44 percent of men.[2,3] The same gap was noted in the UK, where 28 percent of women were reported to use genAI when compared with 43 percent of men.[4] In a further 12 European countries, double-digit differences between women's and men's adoption was found.[5] The figures in the 2025 Appfigures report are starker: nine out of ten ChatGPT users are male across almost all age groups, and 75 percent of ChatGPT mobile app users are men.[6] These numbers are likely the truest reflection of reality on the ground, as they measure actual usage as opposed to the self-reported usage statistics analyzed in most research reports.

One would imagine (hope?) that younger generations of women would be more comfortable embracing emerging technologies than their older counterparts, and that there should therefore be no gap in AI adoption in younger demographic groups. However, that does not appear to be the case. Findings from a top Norwegian business school raise another red flag: female students are 25 percent less likely to report high use of genAI, with high-achieving women being particularly reluctant.[7]

The gulf in AI usage by gender is clearly observable on a global scale; therefore – and perhaps unsurprisingly – we are seeing a similar trend in the legal sector. A 2024 study encompassing legal aid lawyers found that 47 percent of male respondents reported using AI tools for their work, compared to just 17 percent of women respondents. Further, 50 percent of the women said they were not using and did not plan to use AI in their future work.[8] University of Chicago researchers found that 64 percent of male lawyers were using genAI, compared to only 40 percent of their female counterparts.[9]

In a first-of-its-kind gender-lensed industry research initiative, led by She Breaks the Law, The Next 100 Years, and Linklaters, women reported markedly mixed levels of knowledge and uptake regarding AI.[10] While a strong majority recognized AI's importance, only 52 percent of women in the survey described themselves as "very well-informed" about AI technology, with nearly half admitting to limited knowledge or clear gaps in understanding.[11] Paradoxically, women today comprise a slight majority of the legal profession's talent pipeline: 53 percent of lawyers at law firms and 61 percent of in-house counsel are female.[12]

The significance of the AI gender gap

The AI gender gap isn't a theoretical issue – it manifests in everyday professional scenarios. One striking example from *No Woman Left Behind* involved a female junior lawyer who was only able to achieve the right tone of voice when using an AI assistant to write emails when she explicitly asked it to "write as a man". This is a stark illustration of the intertwined issues of bias and exclusion: most AI tools have been trained on data that largely represent the male voice, rather than that of any other gender, and which include the biases inherent within that limited dataset. In this particular example, the AI tool clearly internalized or was trained to recognize the "male" tone as the standard for professional authority.

Another common example is that of image generation tools. A prompt to generate an image of an "international corporate lawyer" will usually produce images of male lawyers in well-tailored, dark-colored suits. If the prompt is modified to explicitly ask for an image of a female lawyer, the output will usually feature a highly sexualized caricature of a woman lawyer.

Additionally, all depictions of "lawyers" produced in these AI-generated images tend to be Caucasian, reinforcing stereotypes and reflecting biases against other minority ethnic groups that might be embedded in the training data.

The upshot of the clear gender bias demonstrated by AI is that many women lawyers rightly question whether these technologies were built for them – and how often, inadvertently or otherwise, the tools they use might even be working against them. This highlights the multi-faceted nature of the problem with AI: women are not using it as much as men and, in its current form, AI is also under-serving women. This is not a niche concern: it carries significant repercussions for not only women professionals, but the legal industry at large. First and foremost is the sheer scale of impact: women make up over half of practicing lawyers in firms and corporate legal departments. The profession cannot fully realize the benefits of AI if the majority of the legal workforce is hesitant about using AI.

On an individual level, women risk falling behind their male peers. AI proficiency is increasingly seen as a "career critical" skill and is rapidly becoming a prerequisite for career advancement. Lawyers themselves recognize how integral AI will be to legal work and, by extension, to their success. In an industry-wide survey by Thomson Reuters, three-quarters of professionals said that they expected AI to have a high or transformative impact on their work in the next few years.[13] The gap in AI adoption could lead to the creation of a "two-tier" system, divided by AI capability. Lawyers who become experts at leveraging AI – to, for instance, automate tedious contract analysis or document review – could dramatically boost their individual productivity and free themselves to focus on higher-value strategic work. Those without such skills (disproportionately women, if current trends persist) may find themselves at a disadvantage, performing more low-value manual tasks and less complex work. Lawyers who cannot confidently use AI will also likely be less attractive to their clients. Over time, this could harden into an invisible barrier to advancement, limiting career progression in an increasingly tech-driven world.

There should be real concern that today's gender gap in AI adoption could translate into tomorrow's gender gap in promotions, pay, and power, widening the existing disparity in senior leadership. Women are already under-represented at senior levels in the profession – for example, only approximately 32 percent of equity partners in major firms are female, despite the fact that women constitute about 62 percent of entry-level associates.[14] Decades of progress toward gender parity in law would be undermined by the introduction of a new "glass ceiling" of algorithms and automation.

Beyond individual careers, there are industry-wide consequences that we need to guard against: if women remain underrepresented among AI users and developers, the technology itself will continue to evolve in a way that neglects or even disadvantages women's needs. A Harvard study noted a worrying possibility of a self-perpetuating vicious cycle: women's underuse of genAI means that these systems are trained on data skewed toward male users, leading to AI outputs and solutions that cater mainly to men; these, in turn, alienate women further.[15] In the legal context, this could manifest in AI legal research tools or document drafting algorithms that reflect male communication styles, male-dominated case datasets, or other subtle biases.

Explaining the gap

Understanding *why* the AI gender gap exists is critical to designing viable solutions for bridging that gap. It will come as no surprise that the causes are complex and multi-faceted, stemming from gender-related social norms, workplace dynamics and the nature of the technology itself.

Time constraints

A persistent theme across the literature is that women lawyers often have less discretionary time to train and learn new technologies like AI, due to disproportionate responsibilities both at work and home. Women lawyers continue to shoulder a greater share of caregiving duties outside the office. They are also frequently tasked with "office housework", responsible for mentoring team members, organizing social events, and the other supporting tasks that keep a firm or legal department running and which are important to fostering a positive work culture but are not career advancing. These responsibilities – both inside and outside the workplace – leave women with less time and energy to attend optional tech training sessions or to experiment with new technologies in their own time.

Researchers also refer to the impact of the "good girl" syndrome, in which women feel pressure to do things "the right way" and not cut corners, unless given explicit approval to use a shortcut. Some women perceive using AI as "cheating" or not "earning" the work product, triggering an internal reluctance to engage with AI tools.

Lack of a seat at the table

Women often have less influence in decisions about technology solutions and their adoption in their workplaces. AI-related strategic initiatives are usually led by senior leadership in a legal practice, as well as by technology departments, both of which are typically majority male. Meanwhile, women are "more busy in the daily duties than in shaping strategic planning".[16] This means that women lawyers may not be as involved in the selection, testing, or rolling out of AI tools as their male counterparts. As a result, the female perspective and their feedback (for example, around issues of bias and accuracy) are not included in the procurement process.

Another consequence is that women may gain less exposure to these tools through the testing phase, when firms run pilots and proofs-of-concepts, which then puts them at a disadvantage when the wider roll-out is implemented. We are left with another self-perpetuating vicious cycle: women are less involved in the strategic decision-making processes and in choosing and testing tools; therefore, implementation programs do not fully consider their needs, which, in turn, makes women even less likely to embrace and adopt the tools.

Career breaks

The pace of change means that any career break or step away from work could lead to missing out on a significant wave of legaltech advancement. If someone left on maternity leave in late 2023 and returned in late 2024, they would have likely entirely missed the introduction of legal AI assistants and other AI tools at their workplace, including all the accompanying training. In addition to the usual challenge of re-integration and client relationship development when returning from a career break, individuals now must also deal with a steep learning curve to catch up with AI tools and pilots that their colleagues are already familiar with. Because women are more likely than men to take extended breaks (after the birth of a child or to accommodate caregiving responsibilities), they are disproportionately at risk of being "left behind".

Bias and trust concerns

Many women lawyers harbor deep concerns about the bias embedded in the AI systems and tools they use, which then dampens their willingness to use them. Unlike early adopter male colleagues, who might approach a new product with enthusiasm and trust, women in law seem to be approaching

AI with justified caution. In the 2024 survey, 43 percent of female respondents reported that they had personally observed bias in the output of the AI tool they had used or tried.[17] Instances of biased outputs included gender or racial stereotypes in AI-generated content, as well as reports of skewed or unfair outcomes in algorithmic tools used for legal tasks. These direct encounters with bias erode trust. For example, if an AI research tool systematically suggests decisions written by male judges over female judges, or an AI-driven recruitment tool shows a pattern of favoring male candidates, women users will justifiably hesitate to rely on those systems.

Female lawyers were also keenly aware of the "black box" nature of many AI models, and this lack of transparency makes it hard to detect or challenge embedded biases. Without confidence that an AI tool will treat their work and their clients impartially, some women professionals are opting not to engage at all.

Accuracy concerns

Users have also expressed worries about the accuracy and reliability of the outputs of AI tools. Lawyers, by nature, are risk-averse and tend – for good reason – to be perfectionists who leave no margin for error. For women lawyers, who may already feel they are under more scrutiny, the prospect of an AI tool making a mistake on their watch is especially chilling. This then ties back to the confidence and reputation of individual lawyers: a man might feel confident that, even if an AI output is wrong, he can defend his choice to use it; a woman, socialized to avoid mistakes, may prefer not to take that chance. The need to thoroughly verify all AI outputs – effectively doubling their workload – then negates the efficiency gains and, thus, the incentive to use the tool. In the survey, some women mentioned needing explicit permission or guidelines before they would feel safe using AI on client work, reflecting a cautious approach to avoid liability or professional missteps.

Higher stakes and harsher penalties

Lastly, an important and nuanced factor is the disproportionate professional penalty women fear they will suffer if an AI-related error does occur. Women in male-dominated professions often feel that they must perform at a higher standard to be taken seriously, and that their mistakes will be remembered more vividly and for a longer period of time. This dynamic also extends to the use of AI: if a male lawyer uses an AI tool that makes a mistake, it might be shrugged off as the technology's fault or a natural consequence of experimentation; if a female lawyer does the same, she may worry it will be perceived as her incompetence. This fear is reinforced by existing gender biases in workplaces: research in other domains has shown that women's errors are often judged more severely or taken as evidence of women's purported lack of ability.[18] Therefore, many women lawyers conclude that the safest course is not to take the risk of using AI on any client work until it is foolproof.

Additionally, even where the results of using AI are accurate and positive, women face a greater competence penalty than their male colleagues. In an experiment with over 1000 software engineers, participants were asked to evaluate Python code that was purportedly written by another engineer, with and without AI assistance. Although the code itself was identical across all conditions, where reviewers believed an engineer had used AI, they rated the engineer's competence as 9 percent lower on average. This competence penalty was more than twice as severe for female engineers, who faced a 13 percent reduction, than for male engineers, who faced a 6 percent reduction.[19] Therefore, even when women use AI, disclosing that they have done so leaves them open to greater scrutiny of their competence and their fundamental abilities – more so than when a man does the same and produces exactly the same results. While this research was performed with a cohort of software engineers, it is not difficult to imagine the same penalty likely exists in the legal sector as well.

The path forward

It is clear that there are many reasons that women are engaging with AI at a slower rate than their male counterparts. If we fail to address this with intent and urgency, this adoption gap could exacerbate existing gender disparities and lead to a two-tiered profession, in which AI proficiency becomes yet another invisible prerequisite for leadership. Leaders of law firms and legal departments, technology vendors, and individual women lawyers all have a part to play in bridging the adoption gap.

Institutional support

With genAI estimated to increase economic output by nearly 20 percent over the next decade, organizations need to recognize AI equity as a business advantage, not a diversity tickbox exercise.[20] The stakes of doing nothing are too high: AI deployment without diverse input can leave blind spots that expose organizations to potential liability and reputational damage. We are already seeing courts penalizing lawyers and firms who have submitted pleadings with hallucinated case citations. Firms that prioritize AI equity will gain compounding advantages over those that fail to do so.

Create space for upskilling and experimentation

Create and protect innovation hours for AI experimentation that count toward billable hour requirements; allocate selected team meetings to group training time; and encourage leaders to model AI adoption for their teams and share use cases. Develop intensive catch-up courses and AI bootcamps for lawyers returning from career breaks during this phase of critical technological transformation.

Make AI training consistent, not a one-off

Move beyond one-off sessions to structured, ongoing programs. Create programs that pair tech-savvy juniors with experienced lawyers who have the critical appraisal skills to train AI tools effectively. This creates a virtuous cycle, in which juniors share technical know-how while seniors provide the judgment to evaluate quality.

Integrate AI skills into career development

Many law societies and bar associations are beginning to recognize AI literacy and responsible AI usage as ethics requirements. Incorporate AI skills into career development frameworks to create a level playing field for all legal professionals. Make AI literacy a factor in promotion decisions, and create specific career tracks for legal professionals specializing in AI and technology.

Build diverse AI talent pipelines

Review your recruitment for AI roles through an intersectional lens to assess whether job adverts are free from gendered or biased language. Use mentoring and sponsoring to create pathways for women into AI leadership, not just filling positions. Set aspirational targets to keep progress measurable.

Establish meaningful governance with real representation

Create AI ethics and governance committees with substantial female and diverse representation – not tokenism, but actual decision-making power. Ensure these committees have the authority to review and approve AI systems before implementation.

Facilitate bias monitoring and reporting

Drawing from emerging regulatory frameworks – like the EU AI Act's requirements for bias detection and mitigation or established models such as NYC's Local Law 144 – conduct regular checks and comprehensive audits on AI tool performance across gender lines. Implement systematic impact assessments to identify potential biases that could affect fundamental rights or lead to discrimination, particularly where AI outputs influence future operations. Create accessible channels for reporting incidents and communicate these widely to build trust and transparency in AI deployment.

Demand better from vendors

Vendor selection matters: demand transparency about model development and bias testing processes. If vendors won't provide this information, treat that as a red flag and dig deeper.

Monitor progress meaningfully

Focus on meaningful engagement, not just usage statistics. Are women using advanced features? Do they have equal representation on governance committees? The goal is not just equal usage, but equal opportunity to develop proficiency and shape how tools evolve.

Vendor responsibility

Vendors can play a significant role in reducing the bias and inaccuracies of output that women are experiencing when they use AI, which is a key blocker to their engagement with and adoption of AI tools.

Equity by design

Vendors must build fairness into AI systems from the start, implementing equity by design, rather than trying to fix problems later. This means having diverse development teams; using diverse training data sources (including, where possible, bias-resistant synthetic data); and conducting continuous monitoring for differential outcomes by gender.

Prioritize transparency

Share training methodologies, bias testing protocols, and accuracy scores so that users can better understand how decisions are made and how reliable they are.

Focus on user feedback
Design mechanisms for collecting and acting on user feedback on bias detection and inaccuracies.

Individual strategies for women lawyers

Just start
Instead of feeling immediately pressured to exhibit expert-level AI skills, begin with simple, high-impact, proven and documented use cases (such as extracting information from large documents, summarizing meetings, or drafting routine communications). Confidence in AI is built with use, and it is important to get past the starting line of the adoption journey.

Prioritize training
Request protected time for AI exploration and prioritize time to participate if formal training programs and opportunities. Document bias and inaccuracies observed, as well as benefits gained, and share that experience with others. This will help to improve the underlying technology while building communities of women users. Stay up to date by subscribing to legal tech publications and following thought leaders.

Leverage the experience advantage
Experienced lawyers are more capable of using AI more effectively than juniors, because they know what "good" looks like. Senior women lawyers, therefore, have an important role to play in training AI tools, providing the female perspective needed for the development of fairer AI systems for the profession.

Lead AI initiatives and contribute to governance
Senior lawyers should volunteer for leadership roles in AI projects within their organizations, including seeking positions on governance and ethics committees. It is important for women's voices to shape the policies and guidelines for AI use in the legal profession, and for junior women lawyers to see that their gender is represented.

Community and collaboration
Women should actively engage with networks like the International Legal Tech Association, She Breaks the Law, and wider gender networks within their

firms and organizations to build community and share experiences and learnings. Invest the time in building relationships with technologists, legal engineers, and data scientists to better understand AI systems, as well as contribute to their further development. Interdisciplinary collaboration leads to more robust and fairer AI systems, and everyone has a role to play.

Conclusions

The research is clear: without deliberate action, AI will not just perpetuate existing inequalities – it will amplify them further. However, the solutions are within reach. Organizations must treat AI equity as a business advantage; vendors must adopt equity-by-design; and women lawyers must start experimenting with AI tools now and advocate for inclusion in governance.

The future of law is being written today, and we have a choice – either to harness this technological disruption to create a more equitable, effective, and just legal profession, or allow it to become yet another advancement barrier for women. It is essential that women's voices and perspectives are at the forefront of this shift, so that AI becomes a catalyst for greater equality, rather than another barrier. The time for action is now.

References

1 Otis N.G., Delecourt S., Cranney K., and Koning R., "Global Evidence on Gender Gaps and Generative AI", Harvard Business School, January 2025. https://www.hbs.edu/faculty/Pages/item.aspx?num=66548

2 Arbanas J., Silverglate P., Hupfer S., *et al*, *Earning trust as gen AI takes hold: 2024 Connected Consumer Survey*, Deloitte, 3 December 2024. See: https://www.deloitte.com/us/en/insights/industry/telecommunications/connectivity-mobile-trends-survey.html

3 Arbanas J., Silverglate P., Hupfer S., *et al*, "Balancing act: Seeking just the right amount of digital for a happy, healthy connected life", Deloitte, 5 September 2023. See: https://www.deloitte.com/us/en/insights/industry/telecommunications/connectivity-mobile-trends-survey/2023/connectivity-mobile-trends-survey-full-report.html

4 Deloitte, *Generative AI: 7 million workers and counting. Digital Consumer Trends UK 2024*, 25 June 2024. See: https://www.deloitte.com/uk/en/Industries/tmt/research/digital-consumer-trends-2024-gen-ai.html

5 The Digital Consumer Trends study conducted in various countries in 2024 revealed genAI adoption gaps of 17 points in Denmark; 12 points in Sweden, Italy, and the Netherlands; 11 points in Belgium; and 10 points in Norway. Additional analysis of a Deloitte European genAI study revealed genAI adoption gaps ranging from 10–15 points in 11 European countries studied (Belgium, France, Germany, Ireland, Italy, the Netherlands, Poland, Spain, Sweden, Switzerland, and the UK). See: Deloitte,

Generative AI: 7 million workers and counting. Digital Consumer Trends UK 2024, 25 June 2024. See: https://www.deloitte.com/uk/en/Industries/tmt/research/digital-consumer-trends-2024-gen-ai.html; *Deloitte, Digital Consumer Trends 2023: Generative AI is all the rage*, 22 November 2023. See: https://www.deloitte.com/no/no/Industries/tmt/research/generative-ai-is-all-the-rage.html; and Corduneanu R., Winters S., Michalski J. et al, "Europeans are optimistic about generative AI but there is more to do to close the trust gap", Deloitte, 10 October 2024. See: https://www.deloitte.com/us/en/insights/topics/digital-transformation/trust-in-generative-ai-in-europe.html

6 Nelson R., *Rise of AI Apps: Key Trends Shaping 2025*, Appfigures, 2025. See: https://land.appfigures.com/rise-of-ai-apps-report-2025

7 Carvajal D., Catalina F., and Isaksson S., "Will Artificial Intelligence Get in the Way of Achieving Gender Equality?", *NHH Dept. of Economics Discussion Paper*, 20 March 2025. http://dx.doi.org/10.2139/ssrn.4759218

8 Chien C.V. and Miriam K., "Generative AI and Legal Aid: Results from a Field Study and 100 Use Cases to Bridge the Access to Justice Gap", *UC Berkeley Public Law Research Paper*, 14 March 2024. https://ssrn.com/abstract=4733061

9 Humlum A. and Vestergaard E., "The Adoption of ChatGPT", *University of Chicago, Becker Friedman Institute for Economics Working Paper*, 14 May 2024. https://dx.doi.org/10.2139/ssrn.4807516

10 This collaborative research involved surveys (in 2024 and 2025) examining women's perspectives and AI adoption patterns, identifying barriers and developing recommendations for bridging the gender gap.

11 Denis-Smith D., Lele P., and Bhandarkar S., *No Woman Left Behind: Closing the AI Gender Gap in Law*, Linklaters, December 2024. See: https://www.linklaters.com/en/knowledge/publications/alerts-newsletters-and-guides/2024/december/03/gender-in-ai-report

12 Solicitors Regulation Authority, "Diversity in law firms' workforce", 3 January 2025. See: https://www.sra.org.uk/sra/equality-diversity/diversity-profession/diverse-legal-profession/

13 Richter M., "How AI is transforming the legal profession", Thomson Reuters, 18 August 2025. See: https://legal.thomsonreuters.com/blog/how-ai-is-transforming-the-legal-profession/#:~:text=Statistics percent20from percent20the percent20Future percent20of,Professional percent20Report

14 Solicitors Regulation Authority, "Diversity in law firms' workforce", 3 January 2025. See: https://www.sra.org.uk/sra/equalitydiversity/diversity-profession/diverse-legal-profession/

15 Otis N.G., Delecourt S., Cranney K., and Koning R., "Global Evidence on Gender Gaps and Generative AI", Harvard Business School, January 2025. https://www.hbs.edu/faculty/Pages/item.aspx?num=66548

16 Denis-Smith D., Lele P. and Bhandarkar S., *No Woman Left Behind: Closing the AI Gender Gap in Law*, Linklaters, December 2024. See: https://www.linklaters.com/en/knowledge/publications/alerts-newsletters-and-guides/2024/december/03/gender-in-ai-report

17 *Ibid.*
18 King M.P., "Why Workplaces Make It Harder For Women To Fail", *Forbes*, 5 March 2025. See: https://www.forbes.com/sites/michelleking/2025/03/04/why-workplaces-make-it-harder-for-women-to-fail/
19 Gai P.J., Hou J., and Tu Y., "Competence Penalty Is a Barrier to the Adoption of New Technology", 11 May 2025. https://dx.doi.org/10.2139/ssrn.5255039
20 Otis N.G., Delecourt S., Cranney K., and Koning R., "Global Evidence on Gender Gaps and Generative AI", Harvard Business School, January 2025. https://www.hbs.edu/faculty/Pages/item.aspx?num=66548

Chapter 4:
Beyond work–life balance: structural constraints and women lawyers' progression

By Claire Rason, executive director, Client Talk

It is often speculated that the reason women leave law and do not become partners is because they "go off and have children". Belying this is an assumption that women still shoulder most of the childrearing and caregiving responsibilities in a family, and an implicit suggestion that the (often disproportionate) work–life balance that partnership in a law firm affords is not compatible with that. This chapter challenges that reasoning by demonstrating that, whilst a lack of work–life balance is indeed something that needs consideration, the assumption that women leave solely because of it is driven by bias. By shining a light on bias and moving beyond it, we can start to challenge not only our own personal biases, but the way in which law firms are led.

The chapter will focus on the challenge that is most often in the spotlight for women: achieving parity at partnership level. Why? The legal profession is increasingly female, and a growing number of women are represented at the lower levels. At the time of writing, in England and Wales, 53 percent of lawyers are women; in the US, men still outnumber women across the profession, but this is shifting in favor or women.[1, 2] However, it is when they rise up the career ladder (or fail to) that cracks emerge: only 32 percent of women are in full-equity partner roles across England and Wales.[3] Challenging the model at the top has benefits that extend throughout the system. Focus on female progression is not new; however, as we gain more insights into what has and has not worked, and what might be behind it all, we can start to do things differently. We can move away from programs intended to fix the women and towards solutions that instead fix the system.

What is stalling women's success?

It is true that working long hours can be seen as part and parcel of a life in law. However, is it really as simple as saying that long hours are the root cause of the gender imbalance that we see at the partnership level?

I started life as a solicitor in London with Herbert Smith Freehills Kramer LLP (hereafter referred to as Herbert Smith). Some 20 years after starting my journey, during which I left legal practice, I decided to go on a hypothetical quest to see if I would have achieved partnership had I stayed. To accomplish this, I followed the journeys of the intake cohort I started with at Herbert Smith in 2002 to see who had eventually risen up to partner or general counsel (GC).

At the beginning, 57 percent of the class of 2002 were women. Some 73 percent of 2002 cohort stayed in law, leaving a population with a roughly equal gender split. However, of the total 2002 cohort, only 23 percent of women achieved the highest level in law, as compared to 59 percent of the men. Whatever way the data were cut, men outperformed women. It was not that women had left private practice or fee-earning work entirely; some did, but so did some men. My research project, *The Class of 2002*, set out to find out why.[4]

The choice to start a family was an aspect that the research explored. The majority of the 2002 cohort had children. It was discovered that, after having children, women found it harder to work the hours required of partnership and were more likely to want more freedom and to have formally changed their working patterns than men. All of this pointed to motherhood and a lack of work–life balance being the root causes of gender imparity at the partnership level. However, all was not as it seemed, and what was happening on the surface masked what was happening at an unconscious level.

Corporate practice: a case study

In *The Class of 2002*, the statistics for corporate practice were poorer than for any other domain of practice: seven men made it to partnership, while only one woman reached the role of GC. This led me to hypothesize that what was going on elsewhere was merely amplified in corporate practice. However, the question remained: why were the outcomes so bad for women in this area of practice?

The broad consensus was that this came down to two things: working hours (the length and unpredictability of those hours) and culture. The culture of corporate practice was said to be particularly difficult for women to navigate, being described a "boy's club", with strong characters that made the working environment challenging. These findings were not specific to Herbert Smith; rather, they were generally applicable to corporate as an area of practice, which seemed to attract so-called "alpha males". This kind of machismo appeared to be synonymous with rainmaking.

The next step was a deep dive into the two variables identified in the case of corporate practice (working hours and culture) to ascertain whether these were truly the cause of the gender disparity within the study cohort and whether they could be extrapolated to law firms more generally.

Were the hours to blame?

While long and unpredictable working hours were cited as a reason for leaving law altogether, only a minority of those surveyed in *The Class of 2002* had actually left legal practice. More women than men agreed with the statement: "The long hours culture at City law firms affected my career choices", with only 20 percent of those female respondents occupying a partner role. Non-partners of all genders were more likely than partners to agree with the statement: "The long hours culture at City law firms affected my career choices." Women were more likely than men to want more freedom and to find the hours "needed to make partner" more difficult to manage after having children.

There are a number of studies that mention the impact of working hours on the career advancement of women. Perhaps the most interesting is one conducted Robin Ely and Irene Padavic, summarized in the *Harvard Business Review*, which argued that the hypothesis that women leave their careers because of having children – dubbed the "work/life narrative" by Ely and Padavic – is actually a mechanism to keep leaders from looking at what is really going on:

> *"Women weren't being held back because of trouble balancing work and family; men, too, suffered from that problem and nevertheless advanced. Women were held back because they were encouraged to take accommodations, such as going part-time and shifting to internally facing roles, which derailed their careers.*
>
> *The real culprit in women's stalled advancement, the authors conclude, is a general culture of overwork that hurts both sexes and locks gender inequality in place. To solve this problem, they argue, we must reconsider what we're willing to allow the workplace to demand of all employees."*[5]

There are plenty of studies which demonstrate the ways in which a 24/7 professional culture harms everyone involved, with many showing how those in the legal profession are burnt out.[6] For instance, the German arm of Linklaters LLP established a scheme in which full-time lawyers could cap their hours to 40 hours a week. More men than women took this up, despite the fact that their participation in this initiative meant that they would therefore be ineligible for partnership.[7] This seems to suggest a desire from practitioners of all genders to break away from the "always on" culture of the legal profession.

Additionally, data from The Law Society of England and Wales[8] seem to support Ely and Padavic's conclusions: a higher proportion of women make use of flexible working opportunities across the profession. However, where business culture is based on rewarding employees for long hours, flexible workers are penalized.

Working long hours vs a 24/7 culture

Working long hours in a role and a 24/7 organizational culture are often conflated. However, *The Class of 2002* invites caution in this regard. A 24/7 culture sets an expectation that employees must always be on call, as opposed to being willing to work longer hours. Additionally, conflation of these terms also limits the discussions around the accommodations often offered to employees. As we have seen, these accommodations are often focused on the ways in which working hours are organized, rather than targeting the expectation of around-the-clock availability.

However, if long and unpredictable working hours were the only barriers to women's success, surely firms in which there is an absence of a 24/7 culture would see gender parity at the partner level? Regional firms in the UK pride themselves on offering an alternative to the organizational 24/7 culture of London firms. However, while working hours are often more manageable outside of London, these regional firms have not achieved parity. This would suggest that something else, aside from the long hours, must be going on in the legal profession.

The other element to culture

The 24/7, always-on approach to work falls underneath the umbrella of culture. Culture is often described as being "how we do things around here". However, I decided to dig deeper, hypothesizing that, in law firms, culture extends to "who does things around here". This is where something interesting emerged.

I sought to identify the traits that the 2002 cohort recognized both in themselves and in partners. The findings were intriguing:

- Men and women see themselves similarly. However, women were more likely to self-describe as "empathetic", while men tended to self-describe as "logical".
- Men and women described partners in similar terms, with some key

differences. Women were more likely to include the words "strong" and "assertive" in their description of partners than men.

- Partners view themselves in a similar way to non-partners. However, while the top-ranking traits were the same, "assertive" was second most prominent trait mentioned by partners to describe other partners.
- "Ambitious" was identified as the top characteristic for a partner by both partner and non-partner men and women.
- The traits present in descriptors of self, yet absent in the descriptors of partners, were "friendly/supportive/empathetic/logical". These were replaced by "ambitious/assertive/strong" as the top partner traits.

What made these findings so interesting is that the descriptors "assertive" and "strong" are commonly associated with men.[9] The traits missing from the 2002 cohort's descriptions of partners – "friendly" and "supportive" – are universally seen as positive in nature, but were replaced with characteristics that possibly speak to a different type of firm culture, such as "ambitious", "assertive", and "strong". These latter characteristics were amplified in the corporate practice.

Studies have described a disconnect between leadership stereotypes and gender stereotypes, which appear to play out in our view of what partners are:

> *" ... effective leadership [competencies] endorse stereotypically masculine attributes, like assertiveness, ambition, and competition, and simultaneously discount stereotypically feminine traits, like collaboration and homemaker. Because masculine stereotypes align with leadership stereotypes, a man is more likely than a woman to be assessed as a potential and competent leader. Feminine stereotypes, in contrast, negatively interact with leadership schema."*[10]

In their research into the demographics of the legal profession, The Law Society of England and Wales describes the way in which the industry often perpetuates narrow definitions of leadership based on characteristics that are traditionally seen as "masculine", such as being decisive, strong, and assertive.[11] This was echoed in *The Class of 2002*.

Unconscious bias at play

As you would have seen demonstrated throughout this book, bias is often hidden – not only to others, but to ourselves. Indeed, this blind spot suggests that we are ill-equipped to recognize our own biases. The Implicit Bias Test, hosted by Project Implicit at Harvard University, is designed to help people identify what biases might be driving them at an unconscious level. One of the biases tested is the work–home conflict, which associates men with pursuing a career and women with the home. Even in instances where someone believes in gender equality or that women can have careers, they might find that, at a subconscious level, their decision-making is affected by this bias. The Implicit Bias Test has consistently demonstrated that this bias exists in the majority of respondents. Only a small percentage showed no bias, or associated men with domesticity.[12] What does this mean? This is an important question to answer, as the choices that men and women make are influenced by it.

This preconception is often compounded with another that we have already alluded to: maternal bias, in which mothers are perceived as less competent or committed because they have children. A study by the American Bar Association found that 67 percent of women lawyers are immediately treated as less committed when they disclose that they are a mother.[13] On the other hand, men are considered more committed when they disclose fatherhood. I am a mother of four, so this particular bias hits hard, especially as I have seen it play out again and again.

Bias compounded: gendered organizations

In the years since completing my research, I have proceeded to explore whether my initial findings were actually an example of a "gendered organization", a concept described in theories positing that organizational structures are not gender-neutral but are, instead, built on a framework of masculinity, which affects female progression by promoting leadership norms that favor stereotypically "masculine" qualities.[14, 15] As with bias, much of this happens at a subconscious level in an organization.

I have tested my initial findings on the perceived characteristics of successful partners; time and time again, I have found that the traits we use to describe partners are male-coded. Younger cohorts of lawyers, both male and female, provide the same answers. This gendered perception of partnership does not appear to shift. At the heart of the notion of gendered organizations is the concept of the ideal worker, which has historically been characterized as a "rational, strong leader, committed to work and unencumbered by family or other responsibilities".[16] This, of course, has historically been a position accessible only to men. Such a conception of the model worker is often deeply rooted in the culture of an organization and is very evident in professional service firms, where the ability to commit to long working hours is often rewarded with leadership. This all points to law firms being an example of a gendered organization. That is a challenging statement to write – and to read.

Choice: why is it easier for women to go and harder for men to leave?

We have discussed the fact that some aspects of organizational culture affect both sexes. Men are burnt out too; they want to have better work–life balance and to spend time with their loved ones. Not all men confirm to the stereotypes that prevail, any more than women do. Furthermore, while I have found some evidence to suggest that women are prevented from reaching the top, I have also found evidence that challenges the assumption that they wanted to get there in the first place. Non-partners reported higher life satisfaction than partners (across both genders), and women felt able to refuse partnership in a way men were not. When I spoke to male lawyers or coaches of male leaders, there was a sense that men tend to step back "once they have made their money" or "when the kids go to university". What was clear is that a lot of this might actually come down to choice. It's probable that the men and women of the 2002 cohort chose different things at different times (the Kaleidoscope Career Model[17] supports this). This might partly be due to changing priorities at different times of life; it also might be due to the perception of choice that each gender holds. In reality, both men and women must make choices impacting their work–life balance that can be critical to their long-term success and allow them to reach their professional goals, such as reaching the C-suite or becoming a partner in a professional firm.

Is it harder for men to turn down partnership? The biases that have been discussed in this chapter apply equally to men, operating in reverse. Men are expected to work; to embody all the stereotypical characteristics of manhood (such as choosing their career over family life or being competitive and assertive as a leader); and to avoid challenging those expectations when making their decisions. When they make decisions, they do so in consideration of the beliefs they are conscious of. However, many of the underlying tenets and assumptions influencing our decisions are not conscious, despite the fact that these will have an impact on the individual and those around them. This is what makes it harder for men to refuse partnership: their internal narrative gets in the way. When men consider whether they should step away from or not to progress in their career, those decisions are questioned – not only by themselves, but by others too.

However, when women choose to step away from or not to progress in their careers, their choices align with existing biases and stereotypes. It is easier for them to turn down or step away from partnership. Furthermore, these individual choices are not questioned. Organizations make it easy for women with caregiving responsibilities to drop out or take detrimental accommodations, because the prevailing model is so inconsistent with their personal lives. The only exception to this is women without caregiving responsibilities, who still face equally significant struggles in their professional lives, because of bias and stereotypes about women that exist more generally.

The opposite can be the case for men. The prevailing model may be equally detrimental to their personal lives, but it is harder for them to leave or take accommodations, due to their self-identification with the organizational zeitgeist. Their professional choices then align with this, and the organizational model remains unchallenged.

Changing workplace culture: a new approach to achieve gender equality in leadership

The core premise of this chapter is that work–life choices are shaped by – and shape in turn – the culture of an organization. Men are often seen as naturally fitting the mold of the ideal worker, which makes it harder for them to question or step away from it. As a result, they are left out of conversations about changing the status quo. When they become a partner, they lead in the way they feel they should, influenced by those male-coded characteristics we associate with leadership. Where the culture of a firm supports the traditional notion of the ideal worker, sponsors or role models champion the same style of leadership, which is why we see the imbalance and obstacles that we do.

Current situation

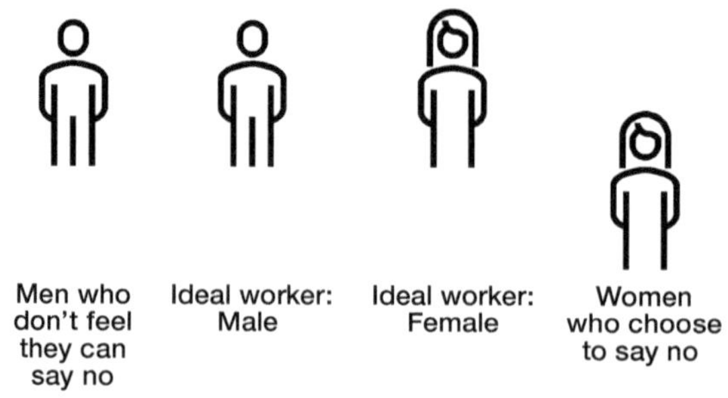

To make real progress on gender equality, firms need to take a hard look at their workplace culture, especially any outdated ideas about what makes a good leader. When leadership is still shaped by traditional notions of the ideal worker (someone who is always available and prioritizing work), it doesn't just hold women back – it limits men too. If we want to keep and grow diverse talent, we need to rethink what effective leadership looks like and create a culture that supports different ways of working and leading. We improve gender equality by changing the internal culture, not by reinforcing traditional working practices. Change of the prevailing workplace culture is needed to enable both men and women to make choices beneficial to both their professional and personal lives. In doing so, firms shift the expectations of what a leader looks like and how they work.

How to address the gender imbalance: two options – which would you prefer?

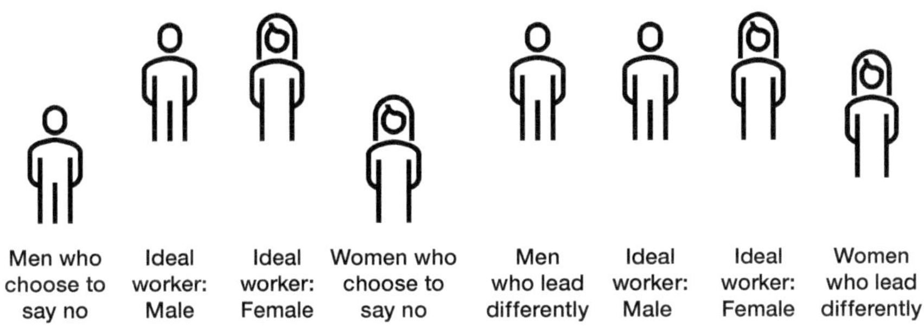

Option 1

Make it easier for men to say no. The prevailing culture "wins", but there is gender parity at leadership level.

This only works if you say that the prevailing culture is the right one for the firm AND it means that you lose out on both male and female talent. This, in time, could provide a challenge to the prevailing culture, but men and women would be involved in reshaping it.

What is seen:
Both men and women choosing to step off the path to partnership.

What isn't seen:
Voices of dissent within partnership.

Option 2

Think about what needs to change in the prevailing culture to make both men and women want to say yes.

In order to achieve this, the work needs to start with thinking about both what the men and women who want to lead differently need. Some of the existing partners might choose to keep their style; others might choose to flex it.

What is seen:
A culture in which different types of leaders can co-exist. Gender parity. Conflict (healthy conflict is not a negative).

What isn't seen:
Women being left behind.

How is change achieved?

The pathway to reaching a new level of equality that enables men and women to lead differently involves:

- Identifying and challenging the principles reinforcing the prevailing culture;
- Working with men who challenge these principles, modelling this behavior to others who do not fit the mold;
- Equally listening to what both men and women need; and
- Equally rewarding inputs and outputs of both men and women that are consistent with the organization's objectives.

What about at an individual level?

Research has found that female self-confidence is impacted by assuming traditionally masculine characteristics in leadership.[18,19] This makes sense: why should women be confident in assuming characteristics that have not served them in getting where they are? These findings provide another argument as to why women might choose not to progress: they might lack faith in their ability to adopt the dominant style of leadership in their organization, or the interest in doing so. If self-confidence is a factor, this aligns with the findings of another study, which demonstrates that coaching is a way to create change in gendered organizations.[20] These studies show that something that can be done by firms to shift the dial. Coaching can increase confidence and challenge the choices that women make. It brings the unconscious into conscious awareness, and can also turn women into agents of change within their organizations.

However, what is important to note is that, to achieve a shift in culture, rather than concentrating on how individuals must behave when they step up to partnership or into another role (as has historically been the case), firms should shift the focus onto the skills individuals already possess, which can be leveraged to achieve results. This shifts the conversation from "You need to be like this" to "How can we leverage who you are when you step up?" However, a note of caution: simply focusing on individual women – something which has been true in many professional service firms when seeking to address gender inequality – risks shifting the blame (and the solution) onto a cog in the machine, rather than targeting the system itself. Furthermore, this is not just about gender – firms must work to embrace all types of diversity. They must take steps to embrace and encourage different leadership styles, which will have an impact on who succeeds in those firms;

this, in turn, will impact the ways in which people perceive their role and ability to fit in, leaving less room for a crisis of confidence.

Looking to the future

One might ask whether the findings from *The Class of 2002* hold good in light of shifts in working models more generally. Things are changing in the ways employees make decisions around family life and work–life balance; this is particularly the case for younger workers during the current recruitment crisis, caused by what has been dubbed the Great Resignation and the phenomenon of "quiet quitting". Both features of the current employment market point to the need for organizations to be more sensitive to the work–life choices employees make and how these impact their perceptions of career success.

The next generations are said not to want to put in the same number of hours and endure the inflexibility experienced by prior generations of lawyers. There is an assumption that things will change (they might) and an acknowledgment that things are improving (they are). These new generations are not afraid to state what they want: their desires about their working life and career trajectory are vocalized in a way that they were not 20 years ago. Firms seem to acknowledge their retention problem, but are currently solving it with eye-watering pay packages, rather than changing the working model. In fact, these salaries may only compound the issue: larger salaries often come with longer hours.

Clients are also increasingly aware of the workplace culture of law firms, which they see as inefficient and outmoded. Clients are increasingly measuring the value of a professional supplier differently – for example, the evaluation of a supplier may include tangible and intangible factors, such as the diversity of the workforce and working conditions. The billable hour model is under strain from clients who do not want to pay it, and technology which no longer supports it. Artificial intelligence means that firms can be more efficient and focus on outputs, rather than inputs.

There are many factors that are creating a perfect storm. When the storm passes, what will be left?

References

1 Solicitors Regulation Authority, "Diversity in law firms' workforce", 3 January 2025. See: https://www.sra.org.uk/sra/equality-diversity/diversity-profession/diverse-legal-profession/#:~:text=Sex-,All percent20lawyers,down percent20from percent200.2 percent25 percent20in percent202021

2 American Bar Association, "ABA Profile of the Legal Profession 2024", 18 November 2024. See: https://www.americanbar.org/news/profile-legal-profession/
3 Solicitors Regulation Authority, "Diversity in law firms' workforce", 3 January 2025. See: https://www.sra.org.uk/sra/equality-diversity/diversity-profession/diverse-legal-profession/#:~:text=Sex-,All percent20lawyers,down percent20from percent200.2 percent25 percent20in percent202021
4 Rason C., "The Class of 2002: Are we treating the symptoms of inequality and not the cause?", 4 March 2022
5 Ely R.J. and Padavic I., "What's really holding women back?", *Harvard Business Review*, March–April 2020. See: https://hbr.org/2020/03/whats-really-holding-women-back
6 LawCare, "Life in the Law 2020/21", 2021. See: https://www.lawcare.org.uk/life-in-the-law/
7 Newman M., "Women in the law: An uphill battle", *The Law Society Gazette*, 30 March 2020. See: https://www.lawgazette.co.uk/women-in-the-law/an-uphill-battle/5103673.article
8 The Law Society, "Trends in the solicitors' profession: Annual Statistics Report 2019", October 2020. See: https://www.lawsociety.org.uk/topics/research/annual-statistics-report-2019
9 Holt C.I. and Ellis J.B., "Assessing the Current Validity of the Bem Sex–Role Inventory", *Sex Roles*, 1998, volume 39, pp. 929–941. https://doi.org/10.1023/A:1018836923919
10 Culture Plus Consulting, "Eliminating Bias From Performance Appraisals", 30 December 2024. See: https://cultureplusconsulting.com/2018/03/10/gender-bias-work-assertiveness-double-bind/
11 The Law Society, "Trends in the solicitors' profession: Annual Statistics Report 2019", October 2020. See: https://www.lawsociety.org.uk/topics/research/annual-statistics-report-2019
12 Intrigued to see where you sit? You can take the test here: https://implicit.harvard.edu/implicit/user/agg/blindspot/indexgc.htm
13 Lee Refo P., "Women's success in legal careers: Lack of advancement is not a 'woman' problem, it's a 'profession' problem", *ABA Journal*, 6 July 2021. See: https://www.abajournal.com/news/article/womens-success-in-legal-careers-lack-of-advancement-is-not-a-woman-problem-its-a-profession-problem
14 Acker J., "Hierarchies, Jobs, Bodies: A Theory of Gendered Organizations", *Gender & Society*, 1990, volume 4, issue 2, pp. 139–158. https://doi.org/10.1177/089124390004002002
15 Acker J., "Gendered organizations and intersectionality: problems and possibilities", *Equality, Diversity and Inclusion: An International Journal*, 2021, volume 31, issue 3, pp. 214–224. https://doi.org/10.1108/02610151211209072
16 Gray D., De Haan E., and Bonneywell S., "Coaching the 'ideal worker': female leaders and the gendered self in a global corporation", *European Journal of Training and Development*, 2019, volume 43, issue 7/8, pp. 661–681. https://doi.org/10.1108/EJTD-01-2019-0011

17 Sullivan S. and Carraher S., "The Kaleidoscope Career Model", *Oxford Research Encyclopaedia of Business and Management*, 28 January 2022. https://doi.org/10.1093/acrefore/9780190224851.013.328

18 Wilkinson F. and Rose S., "An exploration of the relationship between self-confidence and female leadership: The role of workplace coaching in supporting gender equality", *Philosophy of Coaching: An International Journal*, 2022, volume 7, issue 1, pp. 50–64. http://dx.doi.org/10.22316/poc/07.1.04

19 Armour M., "Return of the 'Three Amigos': Applying the Functions of Supervision in the Executive Coaching Context", *Philosophy of Coaching: An International Journal*, 2023, volume 8, issue 8. http://dx.doi.org/10.22316/poc/07.1.04

20 Gray D., De Haan E., and Bonneywell S., "Coaching the 'ideal worker': female leaders and the gendered self in a global corporation", *European Journal of Training and Development*, 2019, volume 43, issue 7/8, pp. 661–681. https://doi.org/10.1108/EJTD-01-2019-0011

Chapter 5:
Rethinking pathways to partnership: advancing equity in a changing profession

By Rachel Khiara, partner, HCR Law

In this pivotal chapter, the focus shifts to the critical crossroads of progress and tradition at which both current and future partners within law firms stand. At a time when diversity, equity, and inclusion (DEI) initiatives are increasingly scrutinized, demonstrating the business case for gender equity in partnership is more compelling than ever. Partnership is the defining milestone in a lawyer's career: it grants influence over strategy, culture, and the direction of the business. However, in the UK's legal profession, it remains the point at which gender inequities often become most pronounced and crystallize. I urge firms to move beyond tokenism and embed gender equity into the fabric of their partnership processes; reimagine the partner track process; challenge the subtle and overt biases that hold women back; and create a profession in which every talented lawyer can reach their full potential.

The legal profession stands at a critical juncture. On one hand, the business case for gender equity has never been clearer: in my opinion, and where supported by firm culture and policy, diverse teams drive better decision-making, foster innovation, and deliver superior profitability. On the other, the traditional pathways to partnership – long shaped by male-dominated norms – continue to present formidable barriers to women. Women make up 62 percent of solicitors with practicing certificates in England and Wales, but only 37 percent of partners are female– and the proportion drops to 28 percent at equity level in firms with 50+ partners.[1,2] Here, where power and profit converge, female representation is even lower.

Clients and regulators alike are applying pressure: corporates expect diverse teams on their panels, and public bodies increasingly require diversity statistics in tenders. Studies confirm that gender-diverse leadership correlates with stronger financial performance, deeper innovation capability, and greater talent retention.[3,4]

Drawing on 25 years in senior roles – ranging from Magic Circle to regional full-service firms, and as founder of a boutique – I explore the ways in which the traditional partner track must evolve through structural reform, cultural shifts, and individual strategies, and how reimagining the partner track process can unlock the full potential of women in law, drive innovation, and enhance firm profitability.

The traditional partner track: a system in need of overhaul

For decades, the partner track in law firms has been defined by a narrow set of criteria: billable hours; client origination; and a relentless commitment to the firm – often at the expense of personal and family life. The focus on billable hours at sustained levels incompatible with long-term wellbeing was – and, in too many firms, remains – the gold standard. Historically, client origination traditionally drew on networks more accessible to men, centered around activities dominated by men, or were held at times out of step with work/life patterns favored by women in the workplace. The need to demonstrate visible devotion to the firm – prioritizing "face time" over actual contribution – are measurables that are incompatible with a value-based culture. These processes often reward presenteeism, long hours, and perpetuate a narrow definition of leadership.

The consequences of this? Talented lawyers moving to in-house teams; attracted to the new consultant-style hub firms; or moving away from the profession after maternity leave. Firms often complain of the loss of their investment in talent; however, even at the most basic level, it is not difficult to identify common factors contributing to women's escape from the legal profession: lack of billable hours; flexibility in working patterns; and no pressure to self-promote. The Solicitors Regulation Authority's (SRA) *Diversity in the Legal Profession* report shows that these criteria are a prime driver of female attrition at the senior associate level, especially between the ages of 30–45 years.[5,6] Firms are losing highly trained lawyers – often to in-house roles or consultant-model firms – because progression is still pegged to outdated definitions of value. Re-evaluating the measurement of talent within the practice of law can only improve retention rates.

Presenteeism and the "ideal worker" myth

Before 2020, presenteeism meant late nights in the office; post-pandemic, it often means "digital presenteeism", defined as instant responsiveness via email, Teams, or other means of online communication. At The Law Society's 2023 post-pandemic practice "Future of Work Conference", speakers advised that firms linking hybrid working to clear performance outputs see a boost in retention among senior female associates.[7] However, without output-focused appraisal, hybrid work merely shifted the venue for overwork from office to home; tokenism remains all too prevalent in firms offering so-called "flexible working" solutions, disadvantaging anyone with significant care-giving duties, which, due to societal norms, disproportionately affects women, whose careers are often subordinated as a result.[8]

In addition, transaction-heavy sectors like banking and corporate M&A still cling to 24/7 availability norms, often requiring pre-pandemic levels of presenteeism, where this is certainly not a necessity. On qualification, many female lawyers continue to gravitate towards residential conveyancing and private client work, where hours tend to be more defined, perpetuating the link between male-dominated sectors in the profession and presenteeism, notably at a senior level.

I recall my early years as an associate in a major City firm, where the unspoken rule was that the last person to leave the office was the most dedicated. I watched talented women, many of whom were mothers, quietly sidelined because they could not (or did not want to) play this game. The result? A loss of talent, perspective, and, ultimately, competitive edge. The "ideal worker" – unencumbered, always available – no longer matches the skill and agility modern clients demand, yet many promotion systems still reward that stereotype.

Reimagining the path: firm case examples from the UK

Change is possible – and it is happening. Ultimately, the new blueprint for a successful forward-looking firm will be the introduction of a "results over hours" policy, shifting the focus from time spent in the office to measurable outcomes: client satisfaction; quality of work; and business development.

Some UK firms have already embedded expanded success criteria, transparent promotion, and flexible structures, with measurable results. Since 2019, partnership appraisals at Clifford Chance no longer score billables as part of the partner bonus appraisal matrix, instead valuing broader contributions such as pro bono, mentoring, innovation, and diversity work.[9] Female partner admissions rose 6 percent within four years in the UK, and up to 9 percent across global regions during that period.[10] Some more innovative firms have implemented a formal sponsorship program. Female mentors encourage a culture within a firm where women are seen and supported, and female mentees result in a more diverse partnership pipeline. Since 2019, Linklaters has run The Women's Leadership Program, which pairs high-potential female lawyers with equity partner sponsors.[11,12] Female partner population in Europe rose from 20 percent to 27 percent by 2025, with a female partner promotion rate of over 40 percent for 5 consecutive years.[13,14]

Across the profession, forward-thinking firms are also experimenting with flexible working arrangements: at Herbert Smith Freehills, as a result of the adoption of their "Agile 60" policy, with no mandated office days, partnership promotions set to reach gender parity in 2026 and female partnership proportions across the firm have risen from 20 percent to 26 percent over 5 years.[15] At a national level, Top 100 firm Moore Barlow has the highest proportion of female lawyers across the firm at 77 percent, which is largely attributable to their approach to flexible working and providing support to female lawyers.[16] Weightmans openly pioneers job-share equity partnerships to keep senior women in key client roles.[17]

These examples demonstrate that intentional structural design – from job shares to open promotion data – is a faster route to equity than awareness campaigns alone.

Respectability politics: the invisible barriers

Formal DEI policies often overlook unwritten rules about how a partner should look, sound, and behave. These respectability politics – documented in Ashley and Empson's ethnographies – still push women toward a narrow male-coded type of professionalism.[18] These respectability politics – which can stifle authenticity and limit career progression – can be as damaging as any official policy.

Sociocultural and psychological dynamics

The pathways to partnership for female lawyers in UK law firms are significantly shaped by sociocultural and psychological dynamics. Social role theory[19] posits that gendered expectations are deeply embedded in society and inform how women are perceived in the workplace. Historically, societies have assigned "communal" traits – such as being nurturing, supportive, and submissive – to women, and "agentic" traits – such as assertiveness, independence, and dominance – to men. In legal environments, this means that female lawyers are often expected to conform to these communal behaviors, which align poorly with stereotypical leadership expectations that favor agentic qualities.

Role congruity theory expands on these principles by proposing that women experience prejudice when pursuing leadership roles that are supposedly incongruent with gender stereotypes.[20] For instance, when a female lawyer demonstrates assertiveness – a quality admired in male leaders – she may be viewed as abrasive or "unfeminine". Conversely, if she is collaborative and supportive, she risks being perceived as lacking necessary gravitas or authority for partnership. This "too soft" versus "too forthright" dilemma highlights the double-bind effect.

The double-bind effect[21] is a particularly stubborn challenge in law firms. Women who display warmth and agreeability may be seen as lacking toughness; in contrast, those who are direct or assertive risk being labelled as unlikable or overly aggressive, facing negative career consequences as a result. Research across corporate and legal sectors consistently shows that women in male-dominated professions must carefully calibrate their communication and leadership styles to avoid these negative stereotypes.[22] For example, seeking a leadership role, advocating for a promotion, or negotiating pay – actions encouraged for men – may prompt backlash against women, reinforcing a cycle of undermined confidence and career stagnation.

Compounding this is the authenticity–performance conflict.[23] Many female lawyers strive to remain authentic to their values and personalities while meeting the expectations of their firms and clients. However, male-dominated cultures may pressure women to behave in ways that conflict with their authentic selves, resulting in emotional dissonance, stress, or even opting out of the partnership track altogether. Research highlights that maintaining authenticity is critical for wellbeing, resilience, and overall satisfaction at work, yet the cost of being one's authentic self often feels higher for women in law, due to prevailing stereotypes.[24]

From dress codes to communication styles, women are often expected to conform to a narrow definition of professionalism. Such outdated views, which are heavily entrenched within the profession, serve no purpose in today's workforce. These expectations are not just frustrating; they are limiting. When women feel compelled to suppress their authentic selves, the firm loses out on the full range of talent and perspective they bring.

Culture change in UK firms

True inclusion requires more than superficial measures, such as diversity quotas or unconscious bias training. It demands a cultural shift – a willingness to question the unwritten rules and to value diverse leadership styles.

Firms must ask themselves: are we promoting people who fit a mold, or those who bring new ideas and approaches? Are we rewarding conformity, or courage?

Some firms are confronting gender norms head on, with structural changes. Herbert Smith Freehills runs a reverse mentoring between senior White male partners and diverse juniors.[25] Baker McKenzie run an inclusive "FeMale Leaders" program to bring female lawyers together for high-level exchange.[26] As a partner myself, I make it a point to mentor and support women in my team, encouraging them to speak up in meetings and develop their own written and oral communication styles. I hope that these women will become the most innovative and effective leaders in the firm.

Post-pandemic working practices and gender equity

The COVID-19 pandemic catalyzed hybrid adoption, but benefits depend on design; hybrid working is by no means a panacea. PwC have found that firms enforcing 3 or more office days had lower female partner promotion rates.[27] In contentious and advisory teams with fully flexible arrangements, gender parity in promotion was achieved more quickly than in transaction-heavy teams where presenteeism persists. The Law Society's Practising Certificate Holder 2022 survey found that 89 percent of women lawyers now work flexibly, which is up from 61 percent in 2019.[28] However, retention and advancement gains were most significant where hybrid policies were universal, eliminating stigma.

Visibility bias remains a risk: without structured work allocation, the most visible lawyers (often office-based) get prime assignments. Some firms mitigate this with transparent assignment systems or rotation models: for example, at Clifford Chance, a "work allocation leader" is an intermediary between associate and partner, accountable for monitoring allocation of high-profile matters, with particular emphasis on ensuring diversity within teams.[29]

The role of clients and firm size: harnessing external and internal pressures

The landscape of gender equity in law is shaped not only by internal firm culture, but also by external pressures – particularly from clients. The difference in gender equity between large, corporate-focused firms and smaller, consumer-facing firms is notable. In larger firms, corporate clients increasingly demand diverse legal teams, creating external pressure for gender equity at the partnership level. These firms are more likely to have formal initiatives aimed at identifying, hiring, and developing female talent. In contrast, smaller consumer firms, lacking such external pressures and resources, often lag behind in promoting women to positions of power.

Corporate clients as catalysts for change

In large, corporate-focused firms, clients are increasingly demanding diverse legal teams. Many now require diversity data as part of their panel selection process. This external pressure has driven significant progress. Where, as a result of DEI policies, women are given more opportunities to lead matters, and their employers have invested in targeted development programs to ensure a robust pipeline of female talent, those who are at a point of considering the direction of their career will remain committed to the firm. These practical strategies advance gender equity. The focus is on leveraging client expectations to drive internal change and ensuring that diversity initiatives are substantive, rather than performative.

The challenge for smaller firms

Smaller consumer firms, lacking such external pressures and often operating with tighter margins, face different challenges. They are less likely to have formal diversity programs and may see gender equity as a "nice-to-have", rather than a business imperative. Often, these firms face succession issues and find flexible working structures more challenging to accommodate. Recognizing these practicalities, change is possible here too. I have advised several boutique firms on low-cost, high-impact interventions: peer mentoring, transparent promotion criteria, and regular diversity audits. Investment in pipeline talent will ultimately alleviate succession issues, and female lawyers who have been supported on their partnership journey will prove powerful guardians of a business able to adapt to changes in the legal sector.

Making value visible

The recognition gap – high performance without equivalent acknowledgement – persists. UK-based research demonstrates that women are less likely to nominate themselves for awards or client pitches.[30] Perhaps the most persistent barrier to partnership for women is the challenge of making their value visible. Despite often working longer hours, producing high-quality work, and achieving impressive results, many women are overlooked for promotion because they do not actively promote their achievements. There are several cultural and psychological factors that contribute to this phenomenon, including modesty norms, fear of backlash, and lack of access to influential networks. Weil Gotshal & Manges LLP specifically addressed this issue in the context of client pitches as part of its Taskforce on Women's Engagement & Retention (TOWER) program, with measurable results: in instances in which female participation increased by 70 percent – notably, where female partner-led pitches rose from 12.8 percent to 20 percent – the female staff retention rate rose from 18.2 percent to 30.6 percent, with positive client feedback on the diversity of the teams. [31, 32]

Strategies for self-advocacy

The solution is not to ask women to "act more like men", but to create environments in which self-advocacy is encouraged and rewarded. In this regard, female lawyers can take ownership. On a practical level, learn to leverage social media to highlight professional accomplishments: share speaking engagements, publications, and case results on LinkedIn and other platforms. Submit to legal directories and include client referees, who will testify to the value delivered. Demonstrating excellence externally speaks louder than recording billable hours. It is good practice to track key metrics, such as matters originated, revenue generated, tenders won, or internal leadership or other initiatives. By quantifying your impact, you build a compelling case for partnership that is difficult to ignore.

Self-advocacy is most effective when combined with strong networks and allies. Seek out mentors and sponsors who will advocate for you in partnership discussions. Join professional organizations, attend industry events, and build relationships with clients. The more people who are aware of your achievements, the harder it is for them to be overlooked.

Lessons learned and the call to action

Reflecting on my own journey, I am struck by both the progress we have made and the distance we still must travel in the legal profession. When I started my career, female equity partners were a rarity, and the idea of flexible working was almost unthinkable. Today, there are more women in leadership than ever before, and the conversation about gender equity is front and center.

However, the barriers remain. Too many talented women are still being held back by outdated processes, unspoken biases, and a lack of recognition.

The profession cannot afford to waste this talent. The business case is clear: firms with diverse leadership outperform their peers, attract better clients, and are more innovative and resilient.

Progress is tangible but reversible. Gender parity at the point of entry to the profession will not change the partner profile without structural reforms and without incorporating transparent, inclusive criteria rewarding value generated, assessed in ways that go beyond outdated metrics. Firms that embrace cultural change by dismantling informal biases will legitimize multiple leadership styles and benefit from the richness that differing perspectives will bring to a firm. Firms that embed these practices show that equity is achievable without sacrificing performance.

Conclusions: building the new partnership model

Rethinking the pathway to partnership is not just a matter of fairness – it is a business necessity. Firms that fail to adapt risk losing top talent, falling behind competitors, and missing out on the proven benefits of diverse leadership teams. The legal profession is changing, but progress is not inevitable. It requires intentional action, courageous leadership, and a willingness to challenge the status quo. By rethinking the pathways to partnership, we can unleash the full potential of women in law and build a profession that is stronger, more innovative, and more just.

References

1 Solicitors Regulation Authority, "Diversity in law firms' workforce", 3 January 2025. See: https://www.sra.org.uk/sra/equality-diversity/diversity-profession/diverse-legal-profession/

2 Solicitors Regulation Authority, "Law firm diversity data tool", 2025. See: https://www.sra.org.uk/solicitors/resources/equality-diversity/law-firm-diversity-tool/

3 Dixon-Fyle S., Hunt V., Dolan K., and Prince S., *Diversity wins: How inclusion matters*, McKinsey & Company, May 2020: See: https://www.mckinsey.com/~/media/mckinsey/featured%20insights/diversity%20and%20inclusion/diversity%20wins%20how%20inclusion%20matters/diversity-wins-how-inclusion-matters-vf.pdf

4 Retention of Women in Law Task Force, *The Business Case for Retaining and Advancing Women Lawyers in Private Practice*, The Law Society of British Columbia, July 2009. See: https://www.lawsociety.bc.ca/Website/media/Shared/docs/publications/reports/retaining-women-business-case.pdf

5 Aulakh S., Charlwood A., Muzio D., Tomlinson J., and Valizade D., *Mapping advantages and disadvantages: Diversity in the legal profession in England and Wales*, Centre for Employment Relations and Innovation and Change, University of Leeds, and

Newcastle University Business School, October 2017. See: https://contact.sra.org.uk/globalassets/documents/sra/research/diversity-legal-profession.pdf

6 Solicitors Regulation Authority, "Diversity in law firms' workforce", 3 January 2025. See: https://www.sra.org.uk/sra/equality-diversity/diversity-profession/diverse-legal-profession/

7 https://diversityandinclusioninlaw.com/attend-future-of-work-conference-19-october-2023/

8 Kumar L., "The Rise of 'Digital Presenteeism': Why Being Online ff Being Productive", We360.ai., 12 March 2025. See: https://we360.ai/blog/the-rise-of-digital-presenteeism-why-being-online-being-productive

9 Walters M., "Clifford Chance drops billable hours for new bonus assessment", *The Law Society Gazette*, 2 May 2019. See: https://www.lawgazette.co.uk/practice/clifford-chance-drops-billable-hours-for-new-bonus-assessment/5070158.article

10 Clifford Chance, "Inclusion: Our FY24 Progress", 2024. See: https://www.cliffordchance.com/content/dam/cliffordchance/About_us/responsible-business/2024/rb-report-inclusion.pdf

11 The Lawyer Network, "Linklaters launches Women's Leadership Programme", 19 September 2012. See: https://www.thelawyer-network.com/news.aspx?n=187&npage=227

12 Linklaters, "Diversity Equity Inclusion", 2025. See: https://www.linklaters.com/en/about-us/diversity-equity-inclusion

13 Linklaters, *Diversity statistics: 2025*, 2025. See: https://lpscdn.linklaters.com/-/media/digital-marketing-image-library/files/02_about-us/diversity-and-inclusion/2025-diversity-report-a4-flyer-final-screen.ashx?rev=538c639c-c5bb-49fd-9124-e97e6d117cdc&extension=pdf

14 Moloney C., "Top firms maintain gender targets in latest partner promotions", *The Law Society Gazette*, 27 March 2025. See: https://www.lawgazette.co.uk/news/top-firms-maintain-gender-targets-in-latest-partner-promotions/5122816.article

15 Wickens Z., "Herbert Smith Freehills uses hybrid working and benefits to improve employee experience", Employee Benefits, 6 March 2025. See: https://employeebenefits.co.uk/total-reward/herbert-smith-freehills-uses-hybrid-working-and-benefits-to-improve-employee-experience/280420.article

16 Baker-Brooker F., "Moore Barlow recognised as top UK law firm for women in latest gender diversity report", *Southern Reporter*, 10 April 2025. See: https://www.thesouthernreporter.co.uk/business/moore-barlow-recognised-as-top-uk-law-firm-for-women-in-latest-gender-diversity-report-5076819

17 Weightmans, "Partner", 2025. See: https://uk.linkedin.com/jobs/view/partner-at-weightmans-4292877326

18 Ashley L. and Empson L., "Understanding social exclusion in elite professional service firms: field level dynamics and the 'professional project'", *Work, Employment and Society*, 2016, volume 31, issue 2, pp. 211–229. https://doi.org/10.1177/0950017015621480

19 Eagly A.H. and Karau S.J., "Role congruity theory of prejudice toward female leaders", *Psychological Review*, 2002, volume 109, issue 3, pp. 573–598. https://doi.org/10.1037/0033-295X.109.3.573

20 Koenig A.M. and Eagly A.H., "Evidence for the social role theory of stereotype content: Observations of groups' roles shape stereotypes", *Journal of Personality and Social Psychology*, 2014, volume 107, issue 3, pp. 371–392. https://doi.org/10.1037/a0037215

21 Gomez R., "The Double-Bind Effect", *The Harbus*, 1 November 2023. See: https://www.harbus.org/post/the-double-binding-effect

22 Gaucher D., Friesen J., and Kay A.C., "Evidence that gendered wording in job advertisements exists and sustains gender inequality", *J Pers Soc Psychol*, 2011, volume 101, issue 1, pp. 109–128. https://doi.org/10.1037/a0022530

23 Spangler S., "McKinsey Legal Podcast, Episode 4: Helen Wan on Creativity and Authenticity", McKinsey Legal Podcast, McKinsey & Company, 22 April 2024. See: https://www.mckinsey.com/featured-insights/in-the-balance/mckinsey-legal-podcast-episode-4-helen-wan-on-creativity-and-authenticity

24 Krengel R., Yee Yau M., and Graf A., *Mapping Systemic Barriers to Equality, Diversity and Inclusion in the Legal Professions*, The Social Change Agency, March 2024. See: https://legalservicesboard.org.uk/wp-content/uploads/2024/08/Mapping-Systemic-Barriers-to-EDI-in-the-Legal-Professions-Final-1.pdf

25 Doraisamy J., "Reverse mentoring will be 'invaluable' for BigLaw firms", *LawyersWeekly*, 27 June 2019. See: https://www.lawyersweekly.com.au/biglaw/25927-reverse-mentoring-will-be-invaluable-for-biglaw-firms

26 Baker McKenzie, "Event Series: FeMale Leaders", 2025. See: https://www.bakermckenzie.com/en/insight/publications/resources/female-leaders

27 PwC, *Annual Law Firms' Survey 2024*, 2024. See: https://www.pwc.co.uk/industries/legal-professional-business-support-services/law-firms-survey.html?WT.mc_id=CT1-PL50-DM2-TR3-LS40-ND13-TTAT3-CN_LawFirmsSurvey-LaunchP

28 The Law Society, "The results are in: how do solicitors feel about their profession?", 6 April 2023. See: https://www.lawsociety.org.uk/topics/research/the-results-are-in-how-do-solicitors-feel-about-their-profession

29 N.A., "The Allocation of Work: Innovative nudges from the field", *The Practice*, January/February 2017. See: https://clp.law.harvard.edu/knowledge-hub/magazine/issues/diversity-nudges/the-allocation-of-work/

30 Donegan H., "Pitch parity: Transforming gender diversity in client pitch activity", fivehundred, 2025. See: https://www.legal500.com/fivehundred-magazine/the-client-side/pitch-parity-transforming-gender-diversity-in-client-pitch-activity/

31 *Weil, Women of Weil: 2023 Progress and Priorities*, 2023. See: https://www.weil.com/publications/women-of-weil-progress-and-priorities/

32 Donegan H., "Pitch parity: Transforming gender diversity in client pitch activity", fivehundred, 2025. See: https://www.legal500.com/fivehundred-magazine/the-client-side/pitch-parity-transforming-gender-diversity-in-client-pitch-activity/

Chapter 6:

Beyond the buzzwords: practical pathways to racial equity and representation in the legal profession

By Hilda Kwoffie, founder and mentor, The BAME Woman in Law

Diversity and inclusion in the legal profession have long been in the headlines; however, for many women lawyers of color, meaningful inclusion remains elusive. Despite the appearance of progress, the numbers reveal persistent inequalities. Representation is slowly improving, but structural barriers still obstruct career progression. Too often, conversations about diversity and inclusion lack action, urgency, and depth.

This chapter will focus on the four pillars that are essential to the professional advancement and wellbeing of women lawyers of color: mentorship, sponsorship, networking, and representation. It also lays out practical steps that the legal profession must take to make racial inclusivity and intersectionality a reality.

Mentorship and sponsorship: a crucial distinction

Mentorship is an established concept in the legal profession, offering opportunities for guidance, support, and professional development. A mentor can help a junior lawyer to navigate office politics and sharpen their legal skills, and provide emotional support and encouragement when their mentee is experiencing the challenges of the job. For many women lawyers of color, especially those who are first-generation professionals or navigating the unwritten rules of large firms, this guidance is invaluable. Mentorship can offer a sense of belonging, and the reassurance that someone else has walked a similar path and survived it.

However, to truly address disparities, we must talk about sponsorship. Sponsorship goes a step further; it is about advocacy. It involves senior professionals using their influence to create opportunities for junior colleagues. Unlike mentorship, sponsorship carries risk for the sponsor, as they are actively putting their name and reputation on the line to advance someone else's career. In a field in which women from ethnic minority backgrounds are still up to six times less likely than White men to make partner in large firms,[1] the need for sponsorship is critical. Without it, many women of color are left to stagnate at mid-level, watching others be ushered forward.

Too often, law firms confuse mentorship and sponsorship or lean too heavily on mentorship initiatives that lack follow-through or accountability. Sponsorship should not be left to chance or goodwill; instead, law firms must institutionalize it, making it a structured, measurable part of leadership responsibilities. Initiatives that match high-potential women lawyers of color with influential sponsors must be embedded in firm culture and linked to performance evaluation.

Networking and representation: the gatekeepers of opportunity

It is often said that success in law is not just about *what* you know, but *who* you know. However, informal networks and unspoken alliances, formed during activities such days at the golf course and drinks after work, remain predominantly White and male. Women of color are frequently left out of these circles, either by omission or design. This exclusion limits their access to key opportunities, high-profile cases, and influential mentors.

In this way, networking becomes more than just a professional skill: it is an access issue. When the rooms where decisions are made remain closed to you, your chances of being selected for client-facing work, speaking opportunities, or leadership development shrink significantly. Law firms must actively create more inclusive environments in which all lawyers feel welcomed into informal and formal networking spaces. That includes reviewing who is being invited to pitch meetings, secondments, or client events.

At the same time, law firms must confront who is typically included in these spaces and who is routinely excluded. Without intentional design, even well-meaning diversity initiatives can reinforce existing barriers. Networking events centered around wine tastings or held in exclusive members' clubs with steep entry fees may be inaccessible or unappealing to many. For women of color, particularly those from working-class backgrounds or with caring responsibilities, such spaces can feel exclusionary and alienating.

Representation also plays a significant psychological role. In a profession where only 8–9 percent of partners come from ethnic minority backgrounds,[2] and where Black women remain particularly underrepresented at senior levels, the absence of role models can reinforce a sense of isolation. When no one in leadership looks like you, it becomes harder to see a future for yourself in the profession. This lack of visibility also means fewer people advocating for your experience and insights at decision-making tables.

In 2021, Ingrid Stephanie Boyce made history as the first Black President of The Law Society of England and Wales. Reflecting on her journey, she acknowledged the isolation that often accompanies trailblazing leadership: "In some roles, I was the only legal expert ... You don't always have that person that you can run to or ask or seek clarification from."[3] Her words underline the emotional and professional weight of being "the only one" in the room; an experience familiar to many women lawyers of color. Boyce has also spoken about the importance of representation, stating: "It's my intention to leave the legal profession more diverse and inclusive than the one I entered."[4] Her presidency has been a powerful symbol of progress, but also a reminder of how far the profession still has to go to ensure that visibility is matched with genuine inclusion and structural support.

Representation is more than a box-ticking exercise; it sends a message about who belongs, who is valued, and who gets to lead. Firms must be intentional about not only hiring women of color, but ensuring their progress is supported at every level.

Tokenism

While some firms are eager to showcase diversity, this often manifests in tokenism, rather than inclusion. Tokenism occurs when organizations spotlight one or two women of color to symbolize progress, while structural issues remain unaddressed. These women are often placed in promotional materials or on diversity panels, without being given real influence or support. As a result, they bear the burden of representing an entire demographic, often without the institutional backing needed to succeed. In 2020, Alexandra Wilson, a young Black barrister, faced repeated microaggressions in court, including being mistaken for a defendant multiple times.[5] Her experience underscores how mere visibility is not enough. Without structural support, these women become overburdened and under-protected.

One overlooked aspect of tokenism is the emotional labor that comes with being "the only one" in a team or firm. These women often become the go-to person for all things "diversity", regardless of their actual role. They are asked to serve on diversity panels, mentor junior staff, and help in fixing systemic issues on top of their billable hours and legal duties. This is not just exhausting; it is unfair. Emotional labor is indeed work, and it must be recognized, compensated, and shared. Firms should avoid overburdening a few visible individuals with the task of fixing systems they did not create. Instead, all leaders should be trained and held accountable for inclusion efforts.

Deconstructing structural barriers

It is not enough to bring women lawyers of color into the legal profession; we must also ask why so many leave. The pipeline leaks at every stage: while increasing numbers of Black and Brown women enter the profession, far fewer rise through the ranks. A Bar Standards Board report revealed that, while 17.3 percent of practicing barristers come from ethnic minority backgrounds, only 10.8 percent of King's Counsel (KC) do.[6] For women, that figure drops further: less than 3 percent of all KCs are women of color.[7]

This gap is not accidental; it is a product of systems that fail to support retention and progression. Bias, both conscious and unconscious, plays a role; so do more insidious factors, like microaggressions, lack of mentorship and institutional inertia. A 2022 report by the Bridge Group, an organization specializing in social mobility, found that employees from ethnic minority backgrounds in law firms were more likely to feel pressure to "fit in" with dominant White, middle-class organizational cultures.[8] For women, this often means managing how they wear their hair, speak, or express emotion, all while under the pressure of performance. Experiences like this are not isolated. The Halo Collective, a UK campaign against hair discrimination, found that 58 percent of Black students experienced name-calling or microaggressions related to their hair.[9]

What does this have to do with progression in law? Everything. If you must dilute your identity to be accepted, the cognitive and emotional toll is immense. Law firms must recognize that inclusivity means creating a culture in which authenticity is not penalized, but embraced.

Intersectionality: when identities intersect

Much of the conversation about diversity in law still treats race, gender, and class as separate categories. However, women lawyers of color navigate multiple, overlapping identities. The barriers they face are not merely additive; they are intersectional. A Black woman may face both racism and sexism in a way that neither Black men nor White women do. Kimberlé Crenshaw, who coined the term "intersectionality", explains this using the metaphor of a traffic intersection: when a crash happens at the intersection of race and gender, it is often unclear which direction the harm came from, but the damage is real.[10] A Muslim woman wearing a hijab may face religious bias layered on top of racial and gendered assumptions; a working-class South Asian woman may not only encounter racism and sexism, but also feel excluded by the unspoken codes of elite legal culture: dress codes, accents, school networks. These nuances matter. Intersectionality is not a buzzword; it's a framework for understanding inequality more precisely.

One of the starkest examples of structural exclusion comes from the judiciary. In 2022, The Law Society reported that only 1.09 percent of judges in England and Wales were Black.[11] Of over 3,000 judges, only a handful were Black women.[12] This lack of representation has consequences not only for aspiring lawyers, but also for the public's trust in the justice system. One notable exception is Dame Linda Dobbs, the first non-White High Court judge in the UK. However, as she has often pointed out, the fact that she remains one of so few speaks volumes. In a profession obsessed with precedent, we must ask: what precedent is being set when only a narrow slice of society is reflected at the top?

The power of collective voice

While institutions have been slow to act, women lawyers of color are increasingly taking matters into their own hands. The rise of peer-led networks, such as The BAME Woman in Law and the Association of Muslim Lawyers, is testament to the power of community. These groups provide safe spaces, mentorship, and advocacy that the mainstream profession often fails to offer. In 2020, following the murder of George Floyd and the global reckoning with racial injustice, legal professionals across England and Wales signed an open letter demanding that the Bar Council and The Law Society do more to tackle systemic racism.[13] This act of solidarity forced conversations that had long been avoided. It also signaled a generational shift: younger lawyers are no longer content with lip service.

So, what does effective inclusion look like? Several firms and organizations have begun to move beyond statements and into measurable action. Linklaters launched a Race Action Plan that includes commitments to double the number of Black partners globally by 2025, implement reverse mentoring, and provide anti-racism training firm-wide. The firm has also set targets to ensure that 15 percent of all new trainees are from Black and minority ethnic backgrounds.[14] The Judicial Appointments Commission has introduced Targeted Outreach programs to encourage more women of color to apply for judicial roles. While outcomes are still emerging, the increased transparency around appointments is a positive step.[15] These initiatives share a common thread: they are intentional, resourced, and linked to accountability. Inclusion cannot be treated as extracurricular; it must be embedded into the DNA of how law firms operate and succeed.

Leadership in law has historically been about conformity: fitting into a mold of neutrality, objectivity, and detachment. However, true leadership in the 21st century must look different: it must be emotionally intelligent, culturally aware, and actively inclusive. That means questioning how leadership potential is defined. Are we rewarding assertiveness over collaboration? Confidence over competence? Are we unintentionally penalizing cultural communication styles that differ from the White, male norm?

Training for senior leaders must go beyond unconscious bias workshops. It must include robust, ongoing education on racial equity, intersectionality, and cultural humility. Leaders must understand how to interrupt bias, sponsor across difference, and foster belonging.

At the core of lasting change is accountability. Law firms are skilled at tracking metrics: billable hours, profitability, client satisfaction. There is no reason that diversity and inclusion cannot be measured with the same rigor. Firms should publish annual diversity reports, disaggregated by race, gender, role, and pay; conduct regular pay gap audits, for gender and race, and publish the results; and set public targets for promotion and retention of women of color and report progress transparently. Moreover, regulators must play a stronger role, mandating regular reporting and setting minimum standards for inclusion training, just as they do for ethics and compliance.

Looking ahead

Inclusion is not a favor done for women of color; it is an imperative for a just, credible legal system. However, inclusion does not happen in a vacuum: it requires allyship. More than that, it requires co-leadership. White men and women in positions of power must see themselves not as passive supporters, but as active co-creators of a new paradigm. This means being willing to give up privilege, declining an opportunity to make space for someone else, and calling out exclusion when it is risky – not just when it is fashionable. It also means investing time, money, and influence to build a profession where every woman, regardless of race or background, can thrive.

The journey towards racial inclusivity and intersectionality in the legal profession is not linear. It is complex, uncomfortable, and ongoing; however, it is also possible. Women lawyers of color have already shown extraordinary resilience, brilliance, and leadership, often despite the odds. The question now is not whether they are ready for the profession – it is whether the profession is finally ready for them.

Let this chapter serve as both a reflection and a roadmap. Let it challenge each of us, regardless of our identity, to examine how we show up, speak up, and stand up for equity. Change does not come from waiting – it comes from doing. The time to act is not tomorrow: it is today.

References

1 Rose N., "SRA: Men six times more likely to be partners than BAME women", *Legal Futures*, 31 October 2017. See: https://www.legalfutures.co.uk/latest-news/sra-men-six-times-likely-partners-bame-women#:~:text="White%20males%20are%20over%20three,the%20case%20for%20BAME%20males

2 Solicitors Regulation Authority, "Race equality in the workplace", 22 April 2025. See: https://www.sra.org.uk/solicitors/resources/equality-diversity/race-equality-workplace/

3 The Law Society, "A presidency like no other: interview with I. Stephanie Boyce", 15 May 2022. See: https://www.lawsociety.org.uk/topics/in-house/a-presidency-like-no-other-interview-with-i-stephanie-boyce

4 Brown D., "Law Society president on diversity: 'We need to move beyond a tick box approach'", LexisNexis, 23 September 2021. See: https://www.lexisnexis.co.uk/blog/future-of-law/interview-i-stephanie-boyce-law-society-president-diversity-inclusion

5 BBC, "Black barrister mistaken for defendant three times gets apology", 24 September 2020. See: https://www.bbc.com/news/uk-england-essex-54281111

6 N.A., "BSB publishes its Annual Diversity at the Bar Report", *The Barrister*, 5 February 2025. See: https://barristermagazine.com/bsb-publishes-its-annual-diversity-at-the-bar-report/

7 Ministry of Justice, "Diversity of the judiciary: Legal professions, new appointments and current post-holders - 2022 Statistics", 13 July 2023. See: https://www.gov.uk/government/statistics/diversity-of-the-judiciary-2022-statistics/diversity-of-the-judiciary-legal-professions-new-appointments-and-current-post-holders-2022-statistics

8 Bridge Group, *Socio-economic Background and Early Career Progression in the Law*, September 2018. See: https://static1.squarespace.com/static/5c18e090b40b9d6b43b093d8/t/5cd180d73cfb160001436429/1557233888333/03+Research+2018+Progression+law.pdf

9 Halo Collective, "We're building a future without hair discrimination", 2025. See: https://www.halocollective.co.uk/

10 Wren A., "Intersectionality: what is it and why does it matter for employers?", Farrer & Co, 4 October 2018. See: https://www.farrer.co.uk/news-and-insights/blogs/intersectionality-what-is-it-and-why-does-it-matter-for-employers/#:~:text=Crenshaw%20uses%20the%20analogy%20of,of%20them%2C%22%20she%20wrote

11 The Law Society, "Over 100 years before the judiciary reflects the Black population in

our society", 26 October 2022. See: https://www.lawsociety.org.uk/career-advice/career-development/solicitor-judges/news/judicial-diversity-forecast-2022#:~:text=Black%20judges%20make%20up%20just,the%20general%20population%20(3.5%25)

12 Gov.uk, *The Lammy Review: An independent review into the treatment of, and outcomes for, Black, Asian and Minority Ethnic individuals in the Criminal Justice System*, 8 September 2017. See: https://assets.publishing.service.gov.uk/media/5a82009040f0b62305b91f49/lammy-review-final-report.pdf

13 Black Solicitors Network, "An open letter to law firm leadership from the Black Solicitors Network", *The Lawyer*, 22 June 2020. See: https://www.thelawyer.com/an-open-letter-to-law-firm-leadership-from-the-black-solicitors-network/

14 Fouzder M., "Linklaters pledges to do better on racial diversity", *The Law Society Gazette*, 23 October 2020. See: https://www.lawgazette.co.uk/practice/linklaters-pledges-to-do-better-on-racial-diversity/5106125.article

15 Judicial Appointments Commission, "Targeted Outreach and Research", 2025. See: https://judicialappointments.gov.uk/targeted-outreach-and-research-team/

Chapter 7:
Beyond barriers: promoting gender and class inclusion in legal education and practice

By Yanthé Richardson, president (2024–2025) and non-executive director, Chartered Institute of Legal Executives, and partner at Foot Anstey LLP

The concepts of intersectionality and inclusivity are critical for understanding and addressing the ways in which access to and progression in the legal profession are shaped by overlapping social and economic factors. Put simply, intersectionality refers to how multiple social and political identities (such as race, sex, gender, class, disability, and educational background) interact to influence a person's lived experience of empowerment or oppression. Intersectionality demands that issues of representation or inequality in the legal profession cannot be addressed by consideration of a single identity (such as gender or class alone) without recognition of the ways in which it interacts with others, such as race or age. For example, a student entering the profession from a low-income background may lack the networks or mentorship needed to secure work experience or entry-level roles – a disadvantage that may be further compounded if they also face racial or gender bias. Relatedly, inclusivity relates to efforts made to ensure that people with diverse backgrounds and identities are supported to enter the legal profession, as well as to be retained and advanced equitably. For example, a law firm committed to socioeconomic inclusivity might consider candidate applications that exclude educational backgrounds; provide financial support for professional qualifications; or specifically recognize the value of non-traditional candidates who bring unique perspectives from their lived experience. Together, intersectionality and inclusivity provide a framework for understanding and addressing socioeconomic disparities within the sector.

This chapter does not ask what women can do better; instead, it challenges the profession to confront systemic exclusion; redesign recruitment, qualification routes, career progression, and firm cultures; and, crucially, to recognize that equity is not charity – it is smart business, as we will see. We will begin by examining current data on socioeconomic diversity across the legal profession, before moving on to apply an intersectional lens to this exploration, identifying systemic barriers and sharing actionable solutions for law firms and institutions. Finally, we will consider what success looks like in a truly inclusive legal profession, and the steps we can take to collectively achieve it.

The current state of socioeconomic diversity in law

The socioeconomic composition of the legal profession in England and Wales remains remarkably static. In England and Wales, there are three main types of qualified lawyer: solicitors, barristers, and chartered legal executives (also known as CILEX (Chartered Institute of Legal Executives) lawyers). Solicitors and chartered legal executives handle case work, providing legal advice, negotiating outside of court, and drafting documents. Where cases require court hearings, solicitors and CILEX Lawyers will often (although there are exceptions) instruct a barrister to represent the client as their advocate. Barristers might provide in-depth written advice, but will primarily spend their time advocating for clients in court. As of summer 2023, data collected by the Solicitors Regulation Authority (SRA) show that, while women made up 53 percent of practicing solicitors, they constituted only 37 percent of partners and 32 percent of full-equity partners.[1] Meanwhile, 57 percent of solicitors reported a professional family background, compared to approximately 37 percent of the general UK workforce, while 21 percent attended fee-paying schools versus the national average of 7.5 percent.[2, 3] Those from more disadvantaged socioeconomic backgrounds accounted for just 18 percent of legal professionals, down from 21 percent in 2015.[4] These imbalances reflect the historic issues that those practicing law have faced, particularly those with intersecting identities, including race, class, sex, and disability status.

In 2020, a study analyzing over 25,000 datapoints, over 60 hours of interviews, and several national datasets revealed career progression delays among certain demographics, with individuals from disadvantaged socioeconomic backgrounds taking nearly two years longer and women taking nearly a year longer to reach partnership than males. Meanwhile, White lawyers were found to progress around two years faster than non-White colleagues.[5] For a profession which exists to serve the public interest, it is essential that these issues are addressed. While individual performance is essential for success, the data reveal that career delays are systemic, not the result of mass individual underperformance.

In contrast, there is evidence to show that firms with diverse leadership see measurable gains. In its 2020 report *Diversity wins: How inclusion matters*, McKinsey found gender-diverse companies were 25 percent more likely to outperform non-diverse competitors financially, while ethnically diverse firms saw a 36 percent uplift.[6]

The aforementioned statistics reflect the solicitor profession, but what of other legal career paths? At the Bar, women now make up over 41 percent of practicing barristers and 58 percent of pupils; however, only 21.1 percent of those reaching the status of King's Counsel (KC) (barristers of at least 15 years' experience, appointed by the Crown as experts in their field) are female.[7] Similarly, barristers from minority ethnic backgrounds account for 17.3 percent of the Bar, but just 10.8 percent of KC; when these characteristics intersect with a working-class background or state school education, the disparity is compounded.[8] The Bar Council has found, for example, that a first-generation Black woman at the Bar is far more likely to experience compounded disadvantages in earnings, progression, and tenancy decisions.[9] When it came to personal characteristics that might not be apparent, the level of declared disability at the Bar had encouragingly risen 0.9 percent to 15.7 percent, which hopefully indicates that respondents do not feel the need to conceal their disability status from their employers.[10]

On the bench, the position is equally stark. The Judicial Diversity Forum's annual statistics recently highlighted this, with all legal exercises completed in the year to 31 March 2025 seeing only 7 percent of applicants from a lower socioeconomic background being recommended for appointment, and less than 1 percent of all judges being Black.[11] Indeed, the current holder of the highest role within the judiciary is the first woman to have held the office since it was created in the thirteenth century.

The position differs greatly when we consider the same datapoints for those who are vocationally qualified. The Chartered Institute of Legal Executives (CILEX) is an organization that offers a flexible route to qualification as a lawyer in England and Wales without the need to attend university (although those with qualifying law degrees can also use this route to qualification, with exemptions). As the 2024–2025 president of CILEX and a practicing lawyer who qualified through CILEX, with 15 years' post-qualification experience, it is only correct that I declare a bias towards a vocational route to qualification, as it has served me greatly in my own legal career. However, the statistics do speak for themselves. The potential for social mobility is evident within CILEX, where qualified professionals are more likely to be the first in their families to enter the legal profession, to come from state school backgrounds, and to have entered law later in life or while working in a different career path, rather than directly from tertiary education.[12] Indeed, CILEX has found that more than 80 percent of its members attended a state school and over two-thirds are women.[13] Some 17 percent of CILEX's members identified as coming from a Black, Asian, or minority ethnic background, and 14 percent reported having a disability.[14] However, despite their qualifications and years of practical experience within their specialism, CILEX lawyers often face limited routes to judicial or senior legal positions when compared to academically qualified solicitors and barristers.[15]

For vocationally qualified lawyers, this is about institutional bias, historical prejudice, and a lack of institutional recognition. In recent years, CILEX has successfully lobbied for the removal of several persistent barriers to its members' progression, with legislative changes opening up more senior judicial positions introduced in 2023. This meant that suitably qualified CILEX lawyers could apply to become recorders (a step on the judicial ladder) and upper tribunal judges for the first time, having previously been unable to apply for posts higher than district judge.[16] The eligibility to be appointed as Crown Prosecutors, one of the final remaining barriers for CILEX lawyers, is being addressed in the Victims and Courts Bill, which has been making its way through the legislative process during 2025.[17] This is important – not only for those vocationally qualified criminal law specialists, who can bring years of experience to these roles, but because it highlights the need to leverage the skills and experience of vocationally qualified lawyers to address the shortage of prosecutors and reduce delays in the court system. This is a clear sign that a diverse socioeconomic legal profession is essential to the provision of access to justice.

I am often asked why I think such a high percentage of CILEX's members are female, and my answer is always that I believe this to be because the route to qualification is truly flexible. It can be started with a secondary school education (although many of our members and trainees are university graduates) and does not adhere to a set timeframe; the cost can be spread, and exams are not condensed into one intense period, but taken at a candidate's own pace. This framework attracts candidates with caring responsibilities; those from disadvantaged socioeconomic backgrounds, who need to be in employment and cannot fund full-time study; and those with other reasons for requiring genuine flexibility.

Understanding intersectionality

The term "intersectionality" was established by academic Kimberlé Crenshaw and refers to the ways in which multiple aspects of an individual's identity (such as their gender, race, class, disability status, sexuality, and more) interact to shape their experiences of privilege and oppression.[18] The statistics we have explored in relation to the Bar of England and Wales have demonstrated that, while progress has been made in improving equity for women in the legal profession, outcomes are far less promising when sex and gender identity intersects with race, disability, or socioeconomic background. Of the 10.8 percent of KC declared as being from minority ethnic backgrounds, just eight are Black women, including the first Black Chair of the Bar Council: Barbara Mills KC.[19, 20]

In her TED talk, *The urgency of intersectionality*, Crenshaw argues: "If you're standing in the path of multiple forms of exclusion, you're likely to be hit by both."[21] The legal profession should engage with the ways in which intersecting identities shape the lived experiences of women in law. Women of color or those who are disabled, LGBTQ+, or from working class backgrounds often face structural barriers, which compound with each intersecting identity. Real-world examples include:

- Black women solicitors being routinely undermined and excluded from informal networks and career progression;[22]
- Disabled women in law encountering inaccessible workplaces and undermining of their ability to handle demanding caseloads or high-pressure environments, despite existing legal obligations around reasonable adjustments;[23]
- LGBTQ+ women, particularly those who are trans or women of color, reporting feeling isolated or unable to be "out" at work, due to fears of professional stigma or subtle forms of exclusion;[24] and
- Working class women, who often do not have family connections in the profession, facing financial and cultural hurdles to accessing training contracts or pupillages, with class-based exclusion often unacknowledged by traditional diversity frameworks.[25]

Drawing an example from my own life, I moved to London in my early 20s on the cusp of qualification as a Fellow of (what was then called) ILEX, having trained in a legal aid practice in a Lincolnshire market town, to take a role at a niche family law firm. As a junior lawyer, I spent a great deal of my time with barristers who were very often Oxbridge-educated and certainly did not sport the Northern accent I carried. As a result, I deliberately and quite rapidly worked to reduce my accent; now, having lived in the south of England for most of my adult life, I am often mistaken as hailing from there. I did this because I felt like an outsider; between my accent, vocational qualification, disadvantaged socioeconomic background, and presented gender, I believed that appearing to "fit in" would better align me with my peers and allow me to be perceived more favorably and taken more seriously. This is not an experience unique to me but, rather, something we can find replicated throughout all levels of the legal profession.

Systemic barriers to inclusion

The disparities revealed by the data we have considered can be attributed to systemic barriers, such as:

- Decreased access to informal networks for those from disadvantaged socioeconomic backgrounds;
- Recruitment processes that favor traditional qualifications, particularly those from elite universities; and
- Rigid career structures that reward presenteeism over performance and offer a severe lack of flexibility for those with caring responsibilities, who are generally women.

When these barriers intersect, they also gain in height: a working class, vocationally qualified woman lawyer with caring responsibilities is facing a barrier three times the height as that of a female colleague with caring responsibilities who is traditionally qualified and with a Russell Group university education. This has led to a severe lack of role models and, importantly, mentors in more senior roles in major law firms and in the judiciary. Junior lawyers and support staff with ambition should be able to look at the partnership or senior staff of their organization and see women who they can relate to, who have overcome these barriers, and who can offer advice and guidance on how they did it.

This is improving, with women making up around 47 percent of lawyers globally and inhabiting 38 percent of leadership roles across jurisdictions, including England and Wales.[26] However, as Dana Denis-Smith OBE, founder of Obelisk Support and the Next 100 Years project, states in the same *Financial Times* article from which these statistics are sourced: "We are at an important crossroads [that] can [either] swing us backwards [or take us] to the next level."[27] Denis-Smith specifically cites the role of the cost of childcare, making the point that, if firms do not pay their staff enough to cover these costs, they are indirectly "forcing" those with childrearing responsibilities to leave.[28] Until very recently, this would have largely been a problem for women employees, who have traditionally carried the burden of childcare. However, recent legislative changes around shared parental leave in the UK and the drive for firms to compete to offer "market-leading" parental leave policies to attract talent will hopefully cause a shift. However, for these initiatives to have their intended effect, men – who have been historically enabled to pursue professional success through women's adoption of caregiving responsibilities – must be willing to contemplate and accept the impact that taking a prolonged absence might have on their careers. Most importantly, employers need to be loud advocates of the benefits of parental leave (especially when it comes to male staff) and be clear with their staff that their career progression will not be impacted. They must also commit to that in practice when the promotion window arrives.

Without clear career pathways, structural change, and sponsorship, women and those from disadvantaged backgrounds or with other intersecting identities will continue to be the higher proportion of employees to face delays to their career progression, as the data have already told us. Gender pay gap reporting, which began in 2017 in the UK for companies employing over 250 staff, has worked to incentivize organizations to close this gap. This initiative has arguably had some impact; however, when examined in conjunction with the pay gaps that exist for staff who are of Black, Asian, or minority ethnic backgrounds, financial equity appears to remain elusive. The Law Society's *Race for Inclusion* research, published in 2020, provides context for this wage disparity in the legal profession, including unfair work allocation, lack of sponsorship opportunities, and an absence of an inclusive culture.[29] Furthermore, The Law Society also found that solicitors of color were more likely to work in smaller firms or less well-remunerated areas of law, being underrepresented in larger firms and sectors like corporate practice, which tend to award higher salaries.[30]

At the heart of this issue lies opportunity. For women from disadvantaged socioeconomic backgrounds, access to education and affordability remain a barrier. In 2020, the Bridge Group found that students from this cohort comprised only 23 percent of those who were accepted onto programs at the top 30 UK law schools; additionally, 80 percent of the top 20 law schools were less likely to accept students from working class demographics on their programs.[31] Even more astoundingly, working class students were required to have higher grades (AAB+) than their peers from more privileged backgrounds.[32]

Even recent decisions made by UK government in 2025 see women further impacted by these systemic barriers, with changes to funding for Level 7 apprenticeships – a vocational, rather than academic, path to qualification – meaning that financial support will only be available for those aged 16–21 years. Legal apprenticeships are impacted by this shift, with those reaching Level 7 often over the age of 21. While firms may choose to privately fund any learners who find themselves at this stage over the age of 21, not all can or will, which could be devastating to those from socioeconomically disadvantaged backgrounds. Apprenticeships, by their nature, are designed to be inclusive and accessible; yet, at the time of writing, the UK government have withdrawn support for learners to become fully qualified lawyers using the levy.

What the system can (and must) do: actionable solutions

Reporting on and recognizing these experiences is essential to the formation of a more inclusive profession. There are opportunities for legal businesses to not only become more responsible employers, but to attract and retain the best talent. This will, in turn, attract clients who will hugely benefit from a range of perspectives and approaches. Firms cannot afford to ignore the importance of a diverse population, with corporate clients now requesting diversity, equity, and inclusion (DEI) data and information on employment of apprentices within tender responses. As our clients become more diverse, they expect the law firms they instruct to be more diverse too, reflecting their own populations. Winning clients by demonstrating your firm's commitment to equity and inclusion is a profitable venture: as mentioned earlier, in an international analysis of public companies, those in the top quarter for ethnic diversity were 35 percent more likely to have financial returns above the national average. Additionally, for every 10 percent increase in gender diversity in senior leadership, profits were found to rise by 3.5 percent.[33]

In my experience, both in my personal journey and the journeys of those I have encountered who come from similar circumstances, lawyers and trainees from diverse backgrounds possess an attribute that is very important in the legal field: resilience. When you have had to overcome personal barriers; juggle full-time work, part-time study, and all the responsibilities at home; and face outdated and prejudicial views of your capability and potential, you develop a high level of resilience. The ability of legal professionals to cope with the pressures and demands of their workloads, handle difficult client interactions, and recover from setbacks is essential. Perseverance in the face of adversity, awareness of your strengths and weaknesses, and the capacity to handle constructive feedback are all skills that resilient staff can offer employers.

However, recognizing the scale of the problem is only the first step. Positive action is needed to improve the current status of DEI in the legal profession. Some actionable solutions include:

- **Consider different routes to qualification**
  Traditional routes into legal practice are not the only ways to create excellent lawyers. Growing recognition of legal apprenticeships (and the levy benefits that accompany them) are a great start to triggering the shift the profession needs to see. In the UK, the introduction of the Solicitors Qualifying Examination provides access to the solicitor profession for non-law graduates; however, other vocational routes to qualification, such as CILEX and the Council for Licensed Conveyancers, produce lawyers of equal capability and – arguably – higher levels of experience and specialism on qualification. These routes require firms to recognize the parity of different routes to qualification; provide adequate financial support for the costs of training; and be clear on the pathways to progression for their alternatively qualified talent. It is paramount that firms ensure alternative routes do not become secondary tracks, which are seen as lesser; rather, they should instead meaningfully invest in this talent and the work they produce by providing the same long-term prospects for partnership and leadership.

- **Reframe career pathways**
  Not everyone wants to be an equity partner. Having recently traversed the promotion pathway to achieve the role of equity partner in a top 100 UK law firm, I can state with authority that the commitment necessary to attaining such a goal must not be focused on just the actual application itself, but distributed across many years through the gradual development of a business case. In many firms, the existing partnership model still often rewards visibility. While this is essential to building relationships, it can also disadvantage those with care-

giving responsibilities. Firms should consider this when drafting career frameworks and promotion criteria. Alternative tracks to equity partnership for those who want to remain employed; adjusted billing expectations for those going through a promotion process and working on a business case; and flexibility in what is considered to be business development are essential to retain and progress diverse talent.

- **Mentorship versus sponsorship**
  Mentoring is always invaluable for juniors in legal practice; however, it is absolutely essential for those whose pathways are non-traditional or who are finding the navigation of law firm politics and career pathways difficult. The importance of access to those who have trodden this path before, lived similar experiences, and can reflect on these honestly and openly cannot be underestimated. Firms who do not yet have a structured mentoring program in place should be taking action to create one without delay.

  Truly active sponsorship can be game-changing for an ambitious individual. Senior leaders who actively promote junior lawyers, talk about them when they are not in the room, and ensure that they are offered the chance to contribute, be visible, and be exposed to development opportunities is essential to the retention of talent. In my career, I have benefited hugely from sponsorship, and I work actively to pass this along to the talent I am lucky to have in my own teams; however, it was not until my firm held a session focused on sponsorship as part of International Women's Day – as recently as 2023 – that I had even heard of the term. When reflecting on this, I realized how much I had benefited from sponsorship, which highlighted to me a real lack of awareness and promotion of sponsorship as an active initiative across the profession. Firms should ensure that their management teams are actively sponsoring their diverse talent.

- **Be accountable to your data**
  Whatever your size of practice, firms should be considering their pay data and examining their wage distribution and career progression timelines by sex, gender identity, ethnicity, disability status, socioeconomic background, and a range of other demographic variables. What proportion of your equity partnership was privately educated? How

many of your partners had parents who were professionals? Your talent needs to see people who share their intersectional identities in the positions they aspire to. If they can see it, they can be it.

- Assess your culture
  Policies, frameworks, success measures, and data alone will not drive improvements: a firm's culture is essential to progress. Investment in inclusive leadership and unconscious bias training, and actively challenging potentially discriminatory attitudes and approaches to both recruitment and promotion, are the bare minimum. While expensive, an external assessment of your firm's organizational culture can be an astute investment when balanced against the risk of reputational damage, lost client work, and the costs of high staff turnover.

What success looks like

What could a properly diverse legal profession look like? A firm in which a noticeable proportion of leaders attended state schools or were the first in their family to enter the legal profession? Is it when a Black woman from a disadvantaged socioeconomic background who works part-time achieving partnership is no longer a unusual occurrence? Or is it vocationally qualified lawyers being recognized as having parity (both of esteem and reward) with their traditionally qualified colleagues when they perform the same role and produce the same results?

These are not unattainable pipedreams, and the legal profession has certainly improved in terms of inclusivity since I joined it in the early 2000s. My own experience – of beginning my career as a trainee legal secretary in a legal aid practice; taking a vocational route to qualification; and eventually becoming an equity partner in a top 100 law firm – is not the only example of its kind. However, it is also not yet commonplace. As we have seen from the data, diversity is key to the success of the profession. Equitable qualification routes, formal sponsorship, redefined partnership criteria for those who seek it, and accountable and inclusive cultures are not optional – they are essential. As law firm leaders, we have a collective responsibility to sponsor and support, remove systemic barriers, act as allies, and adopt an inclusive approach when we consider what success looks like. Without this, the legal profession will not truly reflect the modern society it serves.

References

1 Solicitors Regulation Authority, "Diversity in law firms' workforce", 3 January 2025. See: https://www.sra.org.uk/sra/equality-diversity/diversity-profession/diverse-legal-profession/

2 Solicitors Regulation Authority, "Profession's diversity continues to improve but more to do", 14 December 2023. See: https://www.sra.org.uk/sra/news/press/2023-press-releases/2023-firm-diversity-data-pay-gaps/

3 Bar Standards Board, "BSB publishes its Annual Diversity at the Bar Report", 31 January 2025. See: https://www.barstandardsboard.org.uk/resources/press-releases/bsb-publishes-its-annual-diversity-at-the-bar-report.html

4 *Ibid.*

5 Bridge Group, *Socio-economic background and progression to partner in the law*, 25 September 2020. See: https://www.thebridgegroup.org.uk/news/partner-law

6 Dixon-Fyle S., Vivian H., Dolan K., and Prince, S. *Diversity wins: How inclusion matters*, McKinsey & Company, 19 May 2020. See: https://www.mckinsey.com/featured-insights/diversity-and-inclusion/diversity-wins-how-inclusion-matters

7 Bar Standards Board, "BSB publishes its Annual Diversity at the Bar Report", 31 January 2025. See: https://www.barstandardsboard.org.uk/resources/press-releases/bsb-publishes-its-annual-diversity-at-the-bar-report.html

8 *Ibid.*

9 The Bar Council, *Race at the Bar: Three years on*, 4 December 2024. See: https://www.barcouncil.org.uk/resource/race-at-the-bar—-three-years-on.html

10 Bar Standards Board, "BSB publishes its Annual Diversity at the Bar Report", 31 January 2025. See: https://www.barstandardsboard.org.uk/resources/press-releases/bsb-publishes-its-annual-diversity-at-the-bar-report.html

11 Ministry of Justice, "Diversity of the judiciary: 2025 statistics", 23 July 2025. See: https://www.gov.uk/government/statistics/diversity-of-the-judiciary-2025-statistics

12 Chartered Institute of Legal Executives, *Diversity Report 2023*, 2023. See: https://cilexregulation.org.uk/wp-content/uploads/2023/04/CRL-Diversity-Report-2023.pdf

13 Chartered Institute of Legal Executives, "Ministry of Justice to open up more senior judicial roles to CILEX Lawyers", 11 May 2023. See: https://www.cilex.org.uk/media/media_releases/ministry_of_justice_open_more_senior_roles_cilex_lawyers/

14 *Ibid.*

15 Ministry of Justice, "Diversity of the judiciary: 2025 statistics", 23 July 2025. See: https://www.gov.uk/government/statistics/diversity-of-the-judiciary-2025-statistics

16 Chartered Institute of Legal Executives, "Ministry of Justice to open up more senior judicial roles to CILEX Lawyers", 11 May 2023. See: https://www.cilex.org.uk/media/media_releases/ministry_of_justice_open_more_senior_roles_cilex_lawyers/

17 UK Parliament, "Parliamentary Bills: Victims and Courts Bill", 22 July 2025. See: https://bills.parliament.uk/bills/3968

18 Crenshaw K., "Demarginalizing the Intersection of Race and Sex: A Black Feminist Critique of Antidiscrimination Doctrine, Feminist Theory and Antiracist Politics", *U Chi Legal F*, 1989, issue 1, pp. 139–167. https://chicagounbound.uchicago.edu/cgi/viewcontent.cgi?article=1052&context=uclf

19 Bar Standards Board, "BSB publishes its Annual Diversity at the Bar Report", 31 January 2025. See: https://www.barstandardsboard.org.uk/resources/press-releases/bsb-publishes-its-annual-diversity-at-the-bar-report.html

20 Founder M., "Race report reveals 'limited' progress for black barristers", *The Law Society Gazette*, 5 December 2024. See: https://www.lawgazette.co.uk/news/race-report-reveals-limited-progress-for-black-barristers/5121741.article

21 Crenshaw K., *The urgency of intersectionality*, TED, November 2016. See: https://www.ted.com/speakers/kimberle_crenshaw

22 The Law Society, "Race for inclusion: the experiences of Black, Asian and minority ethnic solicitors", 9 December 2020. See: https://www.lawsociety.org.uk/topics/research/race-for-inclusion-the-experiences-of-black-asian-and-minority-ethnic-solicitors

23 Hirst N., *Legally Disabled – researching into the career experiences of disabled people within the legal profession*, The Law Society, 12 December 2019. See: https://www.lawsociety.org.uk/topics/disabled-solicitors/researching-into-the-career-experiences-of-disabled-people-within-the-legal-profession

24 Mason M. and Vaughan S., "Sexuality at the Bar: An Empirical Exploration into the Experiences of LGBT+ Barristers in England & Wales", *U. of Westminster School of Law Research Paper*, 25 September 2017. http://dx.doi.org/10.2139/ssrn.3043790

25 Progress Together and Bridge Group, *Shaping The Sector: Socio-economic Diversity and Senior Roles in Financial Services*, 2 October 2024. See: https://www.thebridgegroup.org.uk/news/progress-together-launch-data-report-shaping-the-sector-636b4

26 Giusti M., "Gender gap in law at risk of widening amid diversity pullback", *Financial Times*, 25 June 2025. See: https://www.ft.com/content/3a47bb96-f899-4628-af1f-e92a2f18562f?utm_source=chatgpt.com

27 *Ibid.*

28 *Ibid.*

29 The Law Society, "Ethnicity pay gap: what you need to know", 28 January 2025. See: https://www.lawsociety.org.uk/topics/ethnic-minority-lawyers/ethnicity-pay-gap-do-we-really-need-it

30 *Ibid.*

31 Bridge Group, *Admissions to selective UK law schools*, July 2020. See: https://www.thebridgegroup.org.uk/research

32 *Ibid.*

33 Dixon-Fyle S., Vivian H., Dolan K., and Prince, S., *Diversity wins: How inclusion matters*, McKinsey & Company, 19 May 2020. See: https://www.mckinsey.com/featured-insights/diversity-and-inclusion/diversity-wins-how-inclusion-matters

Chapter 8:

Breaking the mold: how neurodiverse women redefine legal excellence

By Pam Loch, chief executive officer and founder, Loch Associates Group

With a sharp rise in diagnoses in recent decades, particularly since the COVID-19 pandemic, much has been made of an "explosion" of neurodiversity. The truth is that, despite many people receiving a diagnosis, statistics show that we are only seeing the tip of the iceberg when it comes to neurodivergence in the workplace. Many neurodivergent people – especially women – remain undiagnosed or choose not to disclose their status.[1] There are also those who are responsible for the care of a neurodivergent loved one alongside pursuing their career; some may even keep this secret, due to the perception that they will not be supported or potentially even penalized professionally.

Whilst there are no data that encompass all possible neurodiverse conditions, trends demonstrate that, while the UK population has grown modestly, diagnoses across the neurodiversity spectrum have risen significantly.[2] This discrepancy could reflect enhanced public awareness, expanded diagnostic criteria, greater health service capacity, and a perception of reduced stigma. However, whatever the reasons behind this spike in diagnoses, it is clear that, because a significant shift has taken place in a relatively short space of time, an evolution in workplace structures and cultures is required to create conditions that support mutually beneficial long-term relationships between employees and employers. This goes beyond merely adhering to a legal requirement: employers must recognize the value that can be gained from a diverse workforce comprising different thinking patterns, experiences, perspectives, and personalities. Organizations must review their approaches to all phases of employee interaction, from recruitment to onboarding, performance management, and exit.

There is only one direction of travel for firms that want to tap into talent, harness their employees' potential, and create workplaces in which people can thrive – one which benefits the bottom line as much as it creates engaged, high-performing, and valued teams. This is needed – not just from a business perspective but, critically, because of the negative impacts on the wellbeing of those neurodivergent lawyers who are not receiving effective support.

To aid firms and practitioners in the development of a more neuroinclusive legal profession, this chapter offers a comprehensive exploration of neurodiversity in the UK's legal sector; contextualizes neurodiversity in policy and clinical contexts; and analyzes research that uncovers how women's presentations have historically been overlooked, the scene is set for why action is needed. This is supported by evidence-based strategies to aid employers to build neuroinclusive practices at every stage of the employment lifecycle, as well as proactive steps that neurodivergent employees themselves can take. The intersectionality of neurodiversity and womanhood is explored, highlighting masking, code-switching, and the additional cognitive load this creates, and offers practical coping strategies for networking, client relationship management, hierarchical interactions, virtual meetings, and large-scale conferences – all of which are integral to legal work. Throughout, this chapter highlights the myriad individual, organizational, and societal benefits that accompany embracing neurodiversity as a profession, moving beyond merely accommodating difference to celebrating it as a source of innovation, resilience, and excellence.

An overview

Employers have both a legal duty and a compelling strategic rationale to support neurodivergent employees. In the UK, under the Equality Act 2010, neurodivergent conditions that substantially affect day-to-day activities are protected as disabilities, requiring organizations to consider and implement reasonable adjustments to remove workplace barriers.[3] Failing to do so not only exposes employers to discrimination claims, but also undermines their duty of care under health and safety legislation, which extends to psychosocial risks, such as unmanaged workload or sensory overload. Beyond compliance, evidence demonstrates that neurodiverse teams outperform homogeneous groups on complex problem-solving, innovation, and pattern recognition – all of which are qualities prized in legal work.[4] By creating environments in which neurodivergent colleagues can contribute their unique strengths without the burden of masking or battling sensory triggers, employers enhance productivity, boost retention, and strengthen their reputation amongst both clients and prospective talent.[5, 6, 7]

From a business perspective, embedding neurodiversity into talent acquisition and development and leadership training aligns with broader diversity, equity, and inclusion (DEI) goals. Firms that cultivate neuroinclusive cultures – through employee resource groups, ally networks, and regular awareness programs, for example – report lower turnover, higher engagement, and a richer pipeline of creative solutions to legal challenges.[8] In such environments, disclosure of neurodivergence becomes less daunting. Although many neurodivergent professionals fear stigma or misunderstanding, disclosure is key to unlocking the adjustments – such as quiet workspaces, flexible hours, and assistive technologies – that enable success.[9] Careful, selective disclosure to a trusted manager, partner or HR professional can be managed via confidential "adjustment passports", ensuring that sensitive information drives practical change without necessitating wider team disclosure.[10] As more individuals feel safe to be open, organizations learn to value cognitive difference as an integrated asset, rather than an awkward exception.

Neurodiversity drives tangible benefits. Studies across sectors link neurodiverse teams to higher levels of innovation, problem-solving, and productivity, with autistic employees in particular demonstrating superior performance in pattern recognition and data analysis tasks.[11,12] Law firms that deliberately recruit and support neurodivergent talent report greater staff retention, an enhanced reputation among clients prioritizing diversity, and a widening pipeline of creative approaches to complex legal challenges. In an increasingly competitive market for legal services, neuroinclusive cultures could confer a distinct strategic advantage.

Conceptualizing neurodiversity: clinical and policy frameworks

The term "neurodiversity" was coined in the late 1990s by sociologist Judy Singer and activists in the autism community as a means of challenging pathologizing narratives of neurological difference and affirming that such differences are inherent variations in the human genome, rather than diseases to be cured.[13] Within this framework, neurodivergent individuals may experience challenges in environments designed for neurotypical cognition, but they also bring distinctive strengths, such as hyperfocus, pattern recognition, inventive problem-solving, resilience, and high attention to detail, all of which can be leveraged to enrich teams and drive innovation.

In UK law, neurodivergent conditions are recognized as disabilities when they have a "substantial" and "long-term" adverse effect on a person's ability to carry out day-to-day activities, per Section 6 of the Equality Act 2010.[14] This protects individuals from discrimination and obliges employers to make "reasonable adjustments" under Section 20, requiring the removal or mitigation of workplace barriers that put neurodivergent employees at a substantial disadvantage.[15] The Act's broad definition of "disability" – encompassing physical or mental impairments – ensures that even less-commonly diagnosed profiles, such as dyscalculia or subthreshold ADHD presentations, fall under its remit if this criterion is met.

In a clinical context, the UK's National Institute for Health and Care Excellence (NICE) publishes guidelines on diagnosing and managing autism and ADHD, emphasizing the need for multidisciplinary assessments that consider developmental history, comorbid conditions, and differential presentations by gender.[16,17] NICE also recognizes that masking and compensatory strategies can obscure clinical features, leading to under-recognition, especially in adult women and girls.

The prevalence of neurodivergent conditions among women in the UK

Accurate information on prevalence is critical for workforce planning, yet many estimates are conservative, due to the underdiagnosis of women with neurodivergent conditions. Studies estimate that approximately 1 percent of the UK adult population is autistic, translating to over 700,000 individuals.[18] Recent studies comparing this estimated prevalence in adults with that of children (1–2 percent) suggests ASD is underdiagnosed in adults, with adult women more likely to remain unassessed or misdiagnosed.[19,20] ADHD prevalence in adults, based on validated screening instruments such as the Adult ADHD Self-Report Scale, is estimated to be around 5 percent, but only a smaller percentage hold a formal diagnosis.[21] Significantly, women screen positive at similar or slightly higher rates than men, but face longer delays before clinical recognition.[22] Dyslexia affects an estimated 10 percent of UK adults, with severe impairment in about 4 percent, while dyspraxia occurs in around 5–6 percent; dyscalculia in 6 percent;[23] and Tourette's/chronic tic disorders in around 0.5 percent of the UK population.[24]

Within the legal profession

When individuals in the UK reach out for legal assistance, they usually start with a solicitor – a legal professional with a potential specialism in certain fields, such as employment, property, or personal injury – who can provide advice, undertake negotiations, and draft legal documents. Should a matter proceed to court, clients are typically represented by a barrister, who advocates on their behalf. The most recent figures from the Solicitors Regulation Authority (SRA) record 172,429 practicing solicitors in England and Wales (53 percent female), and Bar Council data show 18,141 practicing barristers (39.2 percent female).[25,26] Applying conservative neurodiversity prevalence rates suggests roughly 10–12,000 autistic solicitors and more than 10,000 with ADHD among this group, with similar proportions at the Bar. However, underdiagnosis – particularly of women – means self-reporting may capture only 20–30 percent of actual cases, implying a true neurodivergent cohort of 30–48,000 among the roughly 300,000 legal professionals in the UK.[27] Paralegals, legal clerks, and support staff, who total an additional 150–200,000, are likely to mirror these prevalence rates, further expanding the absolute number of neurodivergent individuals in legal settings.

Gendered presentations: the research

Historically, diagnostic criteria for conditions such as autism and ADHD were based on male samples, leading to a default "male presentation" that emphasizes overt repetitive behaviors in autism and hyperactive–impulsive symptoms in ADHD. Women, who more often exhibit the "inattentive" subtype of ADHD or subtler socio-communicative differences in autism, frequently mask their traits to conform to expectations, using strategies such as mimicking peers, memorizing social scripts, and forcing eye contact.[28] While these compensatory behaviors can facilitate momentary social success, longitudinal studies link masking to an increased risk of anxiety, depression, and suicidal ideation, with autistic women reporting higher rates of mental health comorbidities than autistic men.[29]

Research into the "female autism phenotype" highlights distinct patterns: stronger motivation to socialize, yet greater exhaustion from social demands; special interests that may be less stereotypical in nature (e.g., literature, art, or animals, rather than trains or technology); and a higher likelihood of misdiagnosis as borderline personality disorder or anxiety disorders. In ADHD, women often internalize hyperactivity (restlessness, internal agitation) rather than externalizing, leading to missed diagnoses and treatment delays. They also face gendered stigma around inattentiveness being linked to laziness or lack of effort.[30]

Recognizing these gendered differences is key to improving diagnostic pathways, workplace training, and support services that truly reflect women's experiences.

The legal framework: employer duties and carers' rights

In a 2024 survey by Neurodiversikey, 74.6 percent of neurodivergent legal professionals concealed their neurotype to avoid discrimination and 76.3 percent never requested reasonable adjustments, often due to fear of stigma. Of those who asked, 42 percent were refused accommodations.[31]

For both employers and employees, this is alarming, albeit for different reasons. Employees are entitled to support, and failure to provide it can result in claims against an employer, as well as personal and professional harm for the individual concerned. Ensuring that employers are aware of the legal framework is key to a fair and protective employment environment.

The Equality Act 2010

In Section 6, the Equality Act 2010 defines a disability as an impairment that has a substantial, long-term adverse effect on normal day to day activities.[32] Neurodivergent conditions meeting these criteria are classed as a disability, which prohibits direct and indirect discrimination, harassment, and victimization as a result of having a protected characteristic. Under Section 20, employers also have a proactive duty to make reasonable adjustments, which may include modifying working hours, restructuring tasks, providing assistive technologies, altering performance metrics, or redesigning recruitment and assessment processes.[33] Failure to anticipate and implement such adjustments – such as conducting an exclusively panel-style interview or denying the use of noise-cancelling headphones – can constitute unlawful discrimination.

The Employment Rights Act 1996 and Carer's Leave Regulations 2024

From their first day of service, all employees have the right to take reasonable unpaid time off for emergencies involving dependents (a child, spouse, civil partner, parent, or someone who depends on the employee for care) under Section 57A of the Employment Rights Act 1996.[34] Additionally, the Carer's Leave Regulations 2024 grants up to one week's unpaid leave each year to employees who provide or arrange care for a dependent with long-term care needs. This is defined as a mental or physical impairment requiring assistance for at least 28 days.[35] These provisions are especially pertinent to neurodivergent employees who also serve as carers – either for neurodivergent children/adults or older relatives with cognitive impairments – enabling them to manage personal responsibilities without risking disciplinary action or dismissal.

Health and Safety at Work etc. Act 1974

Under the Health and Safety at Work etc. Act 1974, employers have a general duty to ensure the health, safety, and welfare of all employees, so far as is reasonably practicable.[36] This encompasses both mental and physical health. A failure to address psychosocial hazards, such as sensory overload, unmanaged workload, or bullying related to neurodivergent traits, can lead to breaches of these health and safety obligations, resulting in claims, legal redress, and potential reputational damage.

Intersectionality: neurodiversity, gender, and legal culture

The experience of neurodivergent women in law must be situated within the broader context of gendered professional cultures. Law remains male-dominated at senior levels, with partnership and judicial appointments skewed towards men. Women, particularly those with neurodivergent profiles, often face dual pressures: conforming to masculine norms of assertiveness and competitiveness, while navigating gendered expectations around communication style, empathy, and appearance. Masking and code-switching to manage these competing demands incur significant cognitive and emotional cost, contributing to the "double empathy problem", in which both neurotypical colleagues and neurodivergent women struggle to understand each other's perspectives.[37, 38]

Intersectional factors such as race, socioeconomic background, and sexual orientation further shape individual experiences, meaning that a Black autistic woman may encounter different barriers and support needs than a White dyslexic peer. Organizations must, therefore, avoid one-size-fits-all approaches and strive for layered, context-sensitive policies and training.

Fostering neuroinclusivity throughout the employment lifecycle

With an acceptance of the fact that diversity benefits organizations, the development of an effective neuroinclusive strategy that is holistic and proactive and embeds understanding and adjustments at every stage, from recruitment to exit, brings multifaceted benefits. Ensuring that you have the right person in the right seat – with access to effective support that recognizes their limitations, as well as their strengths, and provides alternative solutions – maximizes the likelihood of staff retention, as well as reputational enhancement.

Recruitment and selection

To make interview processes more attractive to neurodivergent talent, employers should begin by auditing job descriptions to ensure they focus on core competencies rather than subjective "soft skills". For example, instead of requiring "excellent interpersonal skills", a role can specify "ability to prepare clear written reports" or "capacity to analyze complex legal texts".

Application processes should support the provision of alternative formats, such as online forms, CV uploads, and video submissions, and communicate clear timelines and next steps to reduce anxiety. During assessment events or interviews, neurodivergent candidates benefit from prior sight of questions to be asked, visual agendas, quiet rooms, and options for remote participation.

Training recruitment teams on neurodiversity reduces unconscious bias. For instance, such training could help recruiters and hiring managers to understand that a lack of eye contact from an interviewee might not be rudeness, but instead a manifestation of a common autistic trait.[39]

Onboarding and induction

A structured induction plan that outlines an employee's schedule, team makeup, workstation layout, and key policies, distributed before a person's first day at work, helps to reduce anxiety. Assigning a dedicated mentor who has received neurodiversity awareness training facilitates regular check-ins on workload, social integration, and any required adjustments.

Training that is delivered in bite-sized modules, supported by written and recorded materials, accommodates diverse learning styles, while a comprehensive welcome pack with office layouts, contact lists, and software tutorials allows self-paced familiarization.

Performance management and development

Traditional, infrequent appraisal meetings can disadvantage neurodivergent employees who process feedback differently or find spontaneous verbal discussion challenging. Instead, managers should collaborate with their team member to agree clear, objective goals with measurable indicators, provide written summaries of review discussions in advance, and offer multiple feedback channels, whether written, in person, or via email.

Regular one-to-one sessions, held at least monthly, ensure emerging issues are addressed early, preventing escalation. Career development can be supported through personalized learning plans, job shadowing, skills workshops, and internal sponsorship, which should all be tailored to diverse cognitive profiles.

Reasonable adjustments in practice

Reasonable adjustments extend well beyond common workplace accommodations, such as flexible working hours or noise-reducing headphones. For instance, task restructuring involves breaking down multi-stage assignments into discrete, time-bounded segments, with explicit deliverables. A complex litigation brief might be divided into stages (legal research, draft skeleton argument, peer review, and final submission), each with its own deadline and check-in. By clarifying priorities and charting incremental progress, this approach reduces overwhelm, supports executive functioning, and builds confidence through visible milestones.

Employers can also leverage assistive technology to support employees with specific neurocognitive profiles. Speech-to-text software empowers those with dyslexia or fine-motor difficulties to draft documents more efficiently, while mind-mapping tools aid individuals with dyspraxia or ADHD in organizing thoughts logically. Screen-reading applications and colored overlays can mitigate visual stress for employees with convergent processing differences, and specialized time management apps, such as digital Pomodoro timers, help neurodivergent users to allocate focused work intervals, track distractions, and visualize remaining time.

Workplace environment modifications are equally critical. Providing low-stimulus workspaces, separate from open-plan hubs, allows employees to retreat from ambient noise, fluorescent lighting, and bustling foot traffic. Adjustable lighting systems enable individuals to set warm or cool tones according to sensory comfort, and decluttered workstations with minimal visual distractions support concentration. Clear signage and wayfinding can help reduce cognitive load when navigating large office complexes, while noise-cancelling headphones offer rapid relief from unpredictable disturbances.

Clear, consistent communication is foundational to neuroinclusive practice. Establishing agreed protocols for conveying instructions, such as preferring concise written briefs over lengthy verbal explanations, dramatically reduces ambiguity and cognitive load. Embedding bullet-point summaries, flowcharts, or annotated diagrams within emails and shared drives ensures that task requirements remain explicit and accessible. Regular check-ins, using written agendas and visual progress trackers, reinforce mutual understanding and create a reliable rhythm for exchange.

Wellbeing support for neurodiverse employees

Legal work is inherently high-pressure, with billable targets, tight deadlines, and adversarial contexts. Neurodivergent employees may be particularly vulnerable to stress, sensory overload, and burnout. A comprehensive well-being program incorporating flexible working policies, including hybrid/home working options, compressed hours, and asynchronous communication norms, will empower individuals to manage energy and focus. Sensory accommodations, such as designated quiet zones, noise-cancelling headphones, reduced fluorescent lighting, and decluttered work areas, mitigate environmental triggers.

Access to neuroinclusive counselling, coaching, and employee assistance programs addresses employees' mental health proactively, while stress management training – mindfulness, time management workshops, and resilience-building courses – fosters coping skills. Regular neurodiversity workshops for leadership and teams cultivate empathy and understanding, reinforcing a culture of inclusion.[40]

Supporting carers of neurodiverse dependents

A significant proportion of neurodivergent professionals, especially women, also serve as primary carers for children, partners, or relatives with neurodevelopmental conditions or cognitive impairments. While the Employment Rights Act 1996 entitles all employees to reasonable, unpaid time off for dependents in emergencies,[41] forward-looking employers go further to acknowledge the ongoing nature of caregiving. By offering a separate allowance of paid carers' leave, organizations recognize the financial and emotional demands of unpredictable care needs.

Flexible scheduling arrangements, including core hours policies, job-sharing and part-time options without career penalty, enable carers to balance work and family responsibilities more sustainably. Partnerships with local childcare or adult social care providers to offer emergency back-up care services alleviate the anxiety of sudden care gaps.

Finally, internal carer support networks and forums, in which employees can share resources, tips, and emotional encouragement, build a community of understanding and practical advice within the organization.[42]

Empowering neurodivergent employees

While employers bear the primary responsibility for fostering inclusion, neurodivergent individuals can take proactive steps to optimize their work experience and career progression.[43] Self-advocacy and disclosure form the bedrock of this endeavor. Preparing a concise, strengths-focused summary of an employee's neurodivergent profile, recommended adjustments, and communication preferences will enable clearer dialog with line managers and HR. Deciding when and to whom to disclose requires weighing personal comfort against potential support benefits, but a well-crafted disclosure plan can pre-empt misunderstandings and facilitate timely accommodations.

Engaging with external networks and mentorship programs can offer critical social and professional capital. Relevant organizations, such as Neurodiversikey®, the Legal Neurodiversity Network, and British Dyslexia Association, provide peer support, role models, and continuing professional development resources that deepen self-understanding and broaden strategies for workplace navigation. Articulation of one's strengths, through which core cognitive attributes are translated into language aligned with organizational goals, helps neurodivergent professionals to demonstrate value. Describing hyperfocus as "exceptional attention to detail" or pattern recognition as "advanced analytical insight" resonates with the competencies sought by law firms.

Boundary management further empowers individuals to protect focus and wellbeing. Blocking out dedicated calendar time for deep work, setting clear preferences for communication channels (for example, email over phone calls), and negotiating protocols for urgent tasks reduce reactive context-switching.

Finally, adopting structured wellbeing practices, including maintaining consistent routines, scheduling brief sensory breaks, using digital tools like Pomodoro timers to segment work, and collaborating with managers to periodically review workload, fosters resilience and sustainable productivity.

Coping strategies for core legal work contexts

Networking and business development

Networking events and business development activities often rely on informal social cues, small talk, and high-stimuli environments. To navigate these settings, neurodivergent lawyers could request attendee lists and consider suggested conversational prompts in advance, which reduces the unpredictability of spontaneous interactions. Arriving early to acclimatize to the venue's layout and noise levels offers a grace period to locate quieter corners or "chill out" rooms. Using business card apps or digital note-taking tools eliminates the manual dexterity and memory demands of writing on tiny cards. Setting personal time limits for how long to spend circulating among groups can help to prevent overwhelm and preserves energy for key connections.

Client relationships

Building and maintaining client trust requires nuanced communication, often across multiple touchpoints. Neurodivergent professionals may find that structuring client interactions with clear, pre-circulated agendas enhances mutual understanding. Following up each discussion with concise written summaries of key points, decisions, and next steps helps to ensure alignment and provides a reference to revisit when memory falters under pressure. Collaborative project management software that visually tracks tasks, deadlines, and responsibilities can further support both lawyer and client in maintaining momentum and accountability.

Hierarchical interactions

Navigating relationships with senior partners, judges, or in-house counsel involves interpreting implicit expectations and managing power dynamics. Preparation strategies include co-drafting meeting agendas where possible, rehearsing talking points with a mentor or trusted colleague, and creating a concise list of questions or clarifications to guide the discussion. After formal meetings, a debrief with a peer or line manager can contextualize feedback, celebrate successes, and identify areas for personal development, reducing anxiety about unspoken evaluations.

Virtual meetings and hybrid work

While remote and hybrid working arrangements can reduce sensory overload, extended screen time and multitasking place significant demands on executive function. Best practices include scheduling shorter meetings with built-in 5-minute breaks, rotating the role of meeting chair to maintain engagement, using chat functions for parallel Q&A, and encouraging participants to share slide decks and notes in advance. Allowing attendees to switch off their cameras when overloaded and recording sessions for later review ensures that important details are not lost to cognitive fatigue.

Conferences and large-scale events

Legal conferences often involve large auditoriums, overlapping sessions, and bustling exhibition halls. To manage sensory and informational overload, neurodivergent attendees might prepare sensory kits, such as ear plugs, sunglasses, and fidget tools, packaged in a small pouch for convenient access. Conference organizers can facilitate inclusion by publishing slide decks and transcripts before presentations, setting up "quiet zones" away from exhibition noise, and scheduling guided mindfulness or stretching breaks between sessions to allow participants to reset and recharge.

Conclusions

Neurodiversity offers a powerful lens through which to reimagine the culture, structures, and practices of the legal profession. For neurodivergent women lawyers, whose cognitive profiles have long been under-recognized and under-supported, the confluence of gendered expectations and neurotypical workplace norms can exact heavy costs in mental health, career progression, and job satisfaction.

By grounding our understanding in robust data, gender-sensitive research, and clear legal obligations under the Equality Act 2010, Employment Rights Act 1996, and Carer's Leave Regulations 2024, employers can move beyond ad-hoc adjustments to systemic neuroinclusive design. From recruitment to onboarding, performance management, wellbeing support, and exit processes, the strategies outlined in this chapter empower both organizations and individuals. Neurodivergent employees, in turn, can amplify these efforts through self-advocacy, network engagement, and strategic boundary-setting, while business development practices that accommodate diverse communication and sensory needs can enhance client service and professional fulfilment.

Ultimately, embracing neurodiversity is not merely an act of compliance or charity – it is a strategic imperative that harnesses a wealth of untapped talent, fosters resilience, and drives innovation. A truly inclusive legal profession is one where neurodivergent women – and all who think differently – are welcomed, valued, and positioned to excel.

References

1 Boocock M., "Two-thirds of workers won't disclose neurodiversity to bosses", Institution of Occupational Safety and Health, 13 October 2023. See: https://iosh.com/about/media-centre/two-thirds-of-workers-won-t-disclose-neurodiversity-to-bosses
2 UKIM Occupational Health & Wellbeing, "Increasing number of adults seeking support for neurodiverse conditions", 28 October 2024. See: https://www.ukim-

oh.com/news/latest-news/increasing-number-of-adults-seeking-support-for-neurodiverse-conditions
3 Equality Act 2010; Sections 6 and 20
4 Mahto M., Hogan S.K., and Sniderman B., "A rising tide lifts all boats: Creating a better work environment for all by embracing neurodiversity", 18 January 2022. See: https://www.deloitte.com/us/en/insights/topics/talent/neurodiversity-in-the-workplace.html
5 *Ibid.*
6 Austin R.D. and Pisano G.P., "Neurodiversity as a Competitive Advantage: Why you should embrace it in your workforce", *Harvard Business Review*, May–June 2017. See: https://hbr.org/2017/05/neurodiversity-as-a-competitive-advantage
7 NeuroBridge, "Why Neurodiverse Teams Run Smoother", 14 April 2025. See: https://neurobridge.co.uk/why-neurodiverse-teams-run-smoother
8 NHS Employers, "Embracing neurodiversity in the workplace", 19 May 2025. See: https://www.nhsemployers.org/articles/embracing-neurodiversity-workplace
9 Advisory, Conciliation and Arbitration Service, "Acas publishes new advice to raise awareness of neurodiversity at work", 31 January 2025. See: https://www.acas.org.uk/acas-publishes-new-advice-to-raise-awareness-of-neurodiversity-at-work
10 Department for Work and Pensions, "Health Adjustment Passport", 12 June 2023. See: https://www.gov.uk/government/publications/health-adjustment-passport
11 Mahto M., Hogan S.K., and Sniderman B., "A rising tide lifts all boats: Creating a better work environment for all by embracing neurodiversity", 18 January 2022. See: https://www.deloitte.com/us/en/insights/topics/talent/neurodiversity-in-the-workplace.html
12 Austin R.D. and Pisano G.P., "Neurodiversity as a Competitive Advantage: Why you should embrace it in your workforce", *Harvard Business Review*, May–June 2017. See: https://hbr.org/2017/05/neurodiversity-as-a-competitive-advantage
13 Singer J., *NeuroDiversity: The Birth of an Idea*, 2017
14 Equality Act 2010; Section 6
15 Equality Act 2010; Section 20
16 National Institute for Health and Care Excellence, "Attention deficit hyperactivity disorder: diagnosis and management", 13 September 2019. See: https://www.nice.org.uk/guidance/ng87
17 National Institute for Health and Care Excellence, "Autism spectrum disorder in under 19s: recognition, referral and diagnosis", 20 December 2017. See: https://www.nice.org.uk/Guidance/CG128
18 National Institute for Health and Care Excellence, "Autism in adults: How common is it?", April 2025. See: https://cks.nice.org.uk/topics/autism-in-adults/background-information/prevalence/
19 National Institute for Health and Care Excellence, "Autism spectrum disorder in adults: diagnosis and management", 14 June 2021. See: https://www.nice.org.uk/guidance/cg142/evidence/full-guideline-pdf-186587677

20 Huang Y., Arnold S.R., Foley K.R., and Trollor J.N., "Diagnosis of autism in adulthood: A scoping review", *Autism*, 2020, volume 24, issue 6, pp.1311–1327. https://doi.org/10.1177/1362361320903128
21 Russell S., Hinwood C., and Fuller C., "Attention deficit hyperactivity disorder (ADHD) Programme update", NHS England, 28 March 2024. See: https://www.england.nhs.uk/long-read/attention-deficit-hyperactivity-disorder-adhd-programme-update/
22 Daisy Chain, "The Gender Disparity in Neurodivergent Diagnoses", 2025. See: https://daisychainproject.co.uk/the-gender-disparity-in-neurodivergent-diagnoses/
23 Williams K., "How Common Are Dyslexia and Dyscalculia in the UK?", Dyslexia UK, 16 January 2025. See: https://www.dyslexiauk.co.uk/how-common-are-dyslexia-and-dyscalculia-in-the-uk-updated-2024/
24 Tourette's Action, "#TourettesWeMatter", 2025. See: https://www.tourettes-action.org.uk/150-touretteswematter.html
25 Solicitors Regulation Authority, "Diversity in law firms' workforce", 3 January 2025. See: https://www.sra.org.uk/sra/equality-diversity/diversity-profession/diverse-legal-profession/
26 Bar Standards Board, "Statistics on Practising Barristers", 2025. See: https://www.barstandardsboard.org.uk/data-and-research/statistics-about-the-bar/practising-barristers.html
27 Saville H., "How the Legal Industry Can Embrace Neurodiversity", Lexxic, 2025. See: https://lexxic.com/blog/how-the-legal-industry-can-embrace-neurodiversity
28 Schuck R.K., Flores R.E., and Fung L.K, "Brief Report: Sex/Gender Differences in Symptomology and Camouflaging in Adults with Autism Spectrum Disorder", *J Autism Dev Disord*, 2019, volume 49, issue 6, pp. 2597–2604. https://doi.org/10.1007/s10803-019-03998-y
29 Jack C., "Masking and Mental Health in Women with Autism", Psychology Today, 26 April 2021. See: https://www.psychologytoday.com/gb/blog/women-with-autism-spectrum-disorder/202104/masking-and-mental-health-in-women-with-autism
30 Bradley S., Parzych I., Platts J., and Powell L., "Understanding and harnessing differences in women with ADHD: A qualitative study", *Neurodiversity*, 2025, volume 3. https://doi.org/10.1177/27546330251317199
31 Neurodiversikey, *Survey results April 2024: Uncharted Territory, v.2.0*, October 2024. See: https://neurodiversikey.com/wp-content/uploads/2024/10/Uncharted-Territory-The-Survey-Results-Report-v.2.0-Oct-2024.pdf
32 Equality Act 2010; Section 6
33 Equality Act 2010; Section 20
34 Employment Rights Act 1996; Section 57A
35 Gov.uk, "Unpaid carer's leave", 2025. See: https://www.gov.uk/carers-leave
36 Health and Safety at Work etc. Act 1974
37 Milton D., "The double empathy problem", National Autistic Society, 2 March 2018. See: https://www.autism.org.uk/advice-and-guidance/professional-practice/double-empathy

38 Milton D.E.M., "On the ontological status of autism: the 'double empathy problem'", *Disability & Society*, 2012, volume 27, issue 6, pp. 883–887. https://doi.org/10.1080/09687599.2012.710008
39 Mahto M., Hogan S.K., and Sniderman B., "A rising tide lifts all boats: Creating a better work environment for all by embracing neurodiversity", 18 January 2022. See: https://www.deloitte.com/us/en/insights/topics/talent/neurodiversity-in-the-workplace.html
40 The Chartered Institute of Personnel and Development, "Neuroinclusion at work", 20 February 2024. See: https://www.cipd.org/uk/knowledge/guides/neuroinclusion-work/
41 Employment Rights Act 1996; Section 57A
42 Chartered Institute of Personnel and Development, "Supporting working carers", 8 June 2021. See: https://www.cipd.org/uk/knowledge/reports/supporting-working-carers/
43 Enlightened Minds, "ADHD In The Workplace: Navigating Challenges In Your Career", 2025. See: https://enlightenedminds.co.uk/adhd-in-the-workplace-navigating-challenges-in-your-career/

Chapter 9:
The leap to law: embracing experience and non-linear careers in the legal profession

By Melanie Arens, founder, Later On Lawyers

The decision to invest one's time, energy, and financial and emotional resources into training towards a new career in and around midlife is invariably a brave and well-considered one. This is particularly the case for those pursuing a path into the ruthlessly competitive, high-pressure, and intellectually demanding legal profession. The aspiration to qualify as a lawyer is often something on which career changers to law have deliberated for a considerable amount of time before they finally take the definitive leap toward achieving their ambition. Many of these profession-pivoters state that their interest in law was sparked early on in life – possibly at high school or during their initial work experience – while, for others, the inspiration occurred slightly later, perhaps via a personal encounter with the legal system, such as during a divorce. That spark of desire to enter the legal world may have taken a back seat over the years in favor of pursuing a more accessible career path or while caring responsibilities took precedence, but it was certainly never extinguished. Common factors that propel mature aspirant lawyers to take the leap include dissatisfaction with their current career path; a desire to test the limits of their potential; and an unfaltering passion for the pursuit of justice. Career changers often express that law is a calling that they feel no other role can quite satisfy.

My encounters with this demographic of late-blooming lawyers have predominately occurred in the course of my own career change journey and through the online community – Later On Lawyers – that I launched in 2024 to connect with and support them. In my experience, there is no typical law convert; rather, they come from a vast array of backgrounds. While the health sector, the armed forces, and financial services are common prior launchpads, some of the more interesting and unexpected professional backgrounds among those in the community include food writers, sporting champions, and directors of musical theatre! Many members have held multiple positions across diverse industries, indicating that legal qualification is just another step on a fluid career journey. With the advent of the major changes to qualification pathways in England and Wales, which will be discussed in this chapter, the scope for alternative work-experienced applicants to enter the legal profession is likely to widen even further.

Notwithstanding the magnetic pull of the legal profession, leaving any career in which one feels proficient and comfortable to start on the bottom rung of a new ladder is undoubtably a daunting experience. Feelings of "imposter syndrome", worries about competing with a younger tech-savvy generation, or fears of encountering ageism in legal recruitment rear readily among this cohort. The women to whom I have spoken are intelligent, dynamic, and often hold positions of seniority in their existing fields – yet they worry immensely about achieving success in law.

The trepidation that mature female candidates experience is easily comprehendible when these law-centric challenges intersect with the systemic adversities affecting women as they leave young adulthood and approach or enter midlife (with midlife generally accepted to start around 40–45 years).[1] This era coincides with a peak in women's caring responsibilities, of both children and older relatives, as well as a tendency to take on more unpaid domestic labor than their male counterparts. It is also the stage of life in which relationship breakdown is more prevalent, with the average age range for females to enter (opposite-sex) divorce proceedings sitting roughly equally across the 35–49 year age range.[2] Financially, women in this cohort are likely to have been impacted by years of the cost-of-living crisis, exorbitant childcare expenses, and consecutive increases in mortgage interest and property rental rates. Women between the ages of 35–44 years are most likely to hold consumer credit,[3] while those aged 35–54 years hold the peak levels of average debt (excluding property debt and student loans).[4] The financial and career setbacks relating to the "motherhood penalty"[5] are becoming well understood, as are the mental and physical challenges pertaining to both perimenopause and menopause itself. Mothers make up 90 percent of single parents in the UK, with their average age being 39.[6]

The socioeconomic profile of women who fall within a broad definition of "mature student" or "career-changer" provides an insight into the foundational barriers they face from the outset of their transition. These women, despite their ambition and demonstrable transferable skills, could easily be forgiven for concluding that the demands of a conversion to law seem insurmountable. The manifestation of these barriers has been revealed in the personal experiences that women in this demographic have shared during my work with them: some alarming tales have included selling the family home to fund academic study or teetering on the point of bankruptcy while trying to secure legal training. I have found it interesting to observe that many in this group state that it is precisely the challenges associated with feminine maturity that have fueled their drive to change the course of their destiny and reach their career change summit.

Statistics from higher education and the legal industry reflect the consistent appeal of the legal profession to women across a broad age spectrum. In 2022, 15,120 UK-domiciled female students were accepted onto undergraduate law courses in England and Wales, compared to 6,440 male students.[7] Regretfully, data demonstrating the number of solicitors admitted to the roll by age and gender have not been made available in recent years, due to the sharp decrease in self-disclosure (94 percent of solicitors who were admitted between 2022–2023 declined to share their personal data).[8] However, previous data have consistently revealed an overall female-to-male ratio within the profession of approximately 60:40 for the last two to 19 years.[9] The average age of admission across both sexes between 2020–2021 was 30 years, and 32.3 percent of the female admissions were aged 30 or above.[10] This predominance of women is reflected across all age categories entering the roll. The trend, and the significant proportion of older qualifiers, underlines the importance of understanding the challenges that mature women face in their journey to practice law.

The career changers with whom I have connected report immense challenges in breaking into the legal profession, often describing it as a system that does not feel designed for them. It is these obstacles that I wish to outline in this chapter, together with some suggested remedies. I have focused on the solicitor pathway, as that is my area of expertise and the predominant career path within the UK's legal profession,[11] but I wish to acknowledge the monumental difficulties faced by aspiring barristers and other legal professionals breaking into the industry. I believe that it is only through a deeper understanding of the barriers faced at the point of entry that the top female talent can be attracted and attained.

Stage 1: The academic qualification process

For approximately three decades preceding September 2021, the traditional path for admission to the roll of solicitors in England and Wales was to attain an undergraduate law degree (an LLB) before completing the postgraduate vocational qualification known as the legal practice course (the LPC) at one of several higher education institutions. LPC graduates were then required to secure a period – ordinarily two years – of recognized training in the legal workplace, commonly known as a training contract (TC). Those that wanted to enter the profession from a non-law degree background were additionally required to take the year-long conversion course known as the graduate diploma in law (the GDL) to be eligible to study the LPC.

This admission process received an immense overhaul in 2021 when the Solicitors Regulation Authority (SRA) replaced this traditional path with "a single, rigorous assessment": the Solicitors Qualifying Exam (SQE).[12] The SRA expressed that its primary objective was to achieve greater assurance of consistent, high standards at the point of admission. It described the existing admission system as expensive and inflexible; as such, it created difficulties for many aspiring solicitors, particularly those from less affluent and diverse backgrounds. Additionally, the regulator wished to develop new pathways to qualification and to promote diversity in the profession by "removing artificial and unjustifiable barriers".[13]

To achieve these objectives, the new admission rules no longer require the next generation of solicitors to hold a qualifying law degree or to complete the GDL: rather, an undergraduate degree in *any* subject – or an equivalent Level 6 qualification – will suffice, in addition to passing the SQE and qualifying work experience (QWE) elements (detailed further below). Candidates must also meet the SRA's character and suitability requirements. The regulator will even consider an applicant's work experience on a case-by-case basis if an equivalent qualification is not held. There can be no doubt that these regulatory changes represent a seismic shift in the spectrum of people to whom a path into the profession is now laid open.

There has been much learning across the legal industry from the first few years of candidates passing through the SQE. The key obstacles I foresee the mature female student facing under the new framework are: achieving success in passing the exams; the scope of the financial risk associated with the SQE; and navigating the plethora of study options available under the new qualification pathway. The three factors are closely interlinked.

Preparation for the SQE pathway

Under the new rules, candidates are not required to study an approved postgraduate preparatory course in advance of sitting the qualifying exams. Therefore, the only upfront cost for the academic stage is that of the exam itself, which is set at an industry-standardized fee: at the time of writing, this is nearly £5,000 for the full SQE.

At first glance, the absence of exam entrance requirements presents the new framework as a more affordable option than the traditional route, in which candidates could expect to incur LPC fees in the region of £8,000–18,000 for the course and assessments and GDL fees of £7,000–12,000 for those requiring the degree conversion. However, many prospective students – not least those taking the giant leap of faith in leaving an existing career and who may have been outside of formal education for some time – conclude it to be too high-risk a strategy to sit the exam without first investing in proper undergraduate and postgraduate legal education and support.

Indeed, aspirant solicitors will find that several major SQE preparation providers are recommending or even *requiring* LLB or GDL completion prior to enrolling on their course, despite it not being mandated by the regulator. Anecdotally, some sectors of the legal market also appear misaligned with the SRA's intentions by demanding these qualifications as a precursor to their TC offer. This points to a reality in which many SQE hopefuls will find themselves factoring the cost of undergraduate legal tuition and SQE preparation into the substantial exam fee, potentially drifting away from any vision of improved economic accessibility to the profession.

In respect of navigating the SQE preparatory products on offer, speculative purchasers will find that a plethora of course providers have flooded the legal education market. These include independent tutors and private companies, together with the higher education institutions that offered the LPC under the traditional route. Their combined offerings present an array of study formats, such as online, in-person, and campus-based options, and provide various starting points throughout the year: an appealing level of flexibility for the time-hungry and responsibility-laden mature applicant. The course options reflect a broad spectrum of price points, currently ranging from approximately £500 to £16,500, which appears to provide scope for some savings for the legal education consumer.

However, one of the major challenges for prospective examinees lies in the fact that the SRA does not regulate, accredit, or endorse these SQE training providers; nor does it approve or oversee the training materials they employ. The regulator does not return exam outcome data individually to the providers, and so candidates cannot conduct outcome-based comparisons of the market. Caution should be exercised in relying on the self-advertised pass rates available, as these are most likely based on data voluntarily returned by the provider's own student populations and may not be entirely representative. Those students wishing to invest in a course that does require an independent quality assurance rating may look to study at a higher education institution in the UK, where assurance is provided by the Quality Assurance Agency for Higher Education through the UK Quality Code for Higher Education.

Financial forecasting for success

A further major consideration for the contemporary law student's purse lies in the overall SQE pass rates that are published by the regulator. This is because, beyond the initial investment outlined above, there is no fee reduction should a student need to re-sit any of the three tranches of SQE exams: currently sitting at nearly £1000 for either of the two SQE 1 exams (both of which students must pass to proceed to SQE 2), and at nearly £3000 for the SQE 2 exam. This represents a very different position to that of the LPC framework, in which individual subject-specific examinations could be retaken at a fraction of this cost, and the entire syllabus could be progressed simultaneously.

The issue of the cost of resits is not a moot one when one explores the pass rates flowing from the SQE thus far. At the time of writing, average pass rates for SQE 1 range between 48–60 percent for all candidates passing on their first attempt, and between 69–81 percent for all candidates passing the SQE 2.[14] Commentators in the field have been keen to highlight that, as candidates can only sit the SQE 2 by first passing the SQE 1, the adjusted average pass rate for those passing the entire SQE at first attempt is nearer a concerningly low 42 percent.[15]

Sadly, this picture does not improve for the focus group of this chapter when one differentiates the pass rate data by age and gender. The SRA statistical reports show a downward trend in the percentage of pass rates by age for those sitting the exams: for SQE 1, this trend is consistent in age groupings from age 25 onwards; for SQE 2, it is consistent across all age groups examined. When considering gender, the reports demonstrate that women consistently underperformed on average when compared to their male counterparts in the SQE 1 exams (save for the July 2022 cohort); however, more encouragingly, women perform the same or marginally better on average than males in all SQE 2 exams taken thus far.[16]

While the SQE 2 results for women are promising, one cannot disregard the barrier to progress that the weaker SQE 1 results will create for female entrants, given that latter is the gatekeeper to former. The legal industry –

and, specifically, the SRA – will urgently need to analyze and unpack these differential SQE outcomes by age and gender if it is to truly realize a goal of multigenerational female diversity in the profession. The consistent reduction in the proportion of candidates sitting the SQE by age grouping, and the poor pass rates for those resitting exams, is also worthy of consideration. Hopefully, the forthcoming SRA-commissioned independent reviews of the SQE will prove vital in identifying the issues at play, and the matter must remain high on the regulator's agenda until it is better understood.

Career switchers have also been keen to highlight the additional financial and logistical implications arising from the fact that the exams are held in centralized test centers throughout England and Wales, and not at the site of the educational provider. For some examinees, this has resulted in needing to travel to a location many miles from home and incurring expenses related to childcare, travel, and overnight accommodation. The cumulative financial burden presented by the SQE can serve to create an overwhelming pressure on students to succeed on their first attempt. As such, the structure of the new scheme risks deterring capable would-be mature applicants from the profession entirely, based on financial risk forecasting and practicalities alone – the definition of "unjustifiable barriers".

Access to funding

A further consequence of the poor first attempt SQE pass rates is law firms' disinclination to sponsor the SQE for its incoming trainees. Many firms already request evidence of a self-funded SQE1 pass result as a criterion for their TC or QWE offer, presumably for this reason. For career changers, a demise in sponsorship opportunities would reflect a real detriment, particularly because the SQE and its preparatory courses (unlike the LPC before it) are not certified educational qualifications for the purposes of accessing the UK government's student loan financing. Those unable to self-fund or secure a private personal loan risk exclusion from the profession, based solely on their economic circumstances.

To counterbalance this funding hurdle, some higher education institutions have enabled candidates to access student finance by incorporating the SQE preparatory element into their Level 7 (master's degree) course options. While this funding may present as a lifeline for many candidates, it will not assist those that have already completed an equivalent Level 7 qualification (who are more likely to sit in the maturer age bracket), as they are ineligible for further student finance. For the finance-compromised and time-depleted students within the career change community, the idea of taking on additional student debt, as well as further academic study that is superfluous to the new solicitor qualification, may prove less than appealing. That said, education providers are proving increasingly creative in their efforts to circumvent financial barriers, such as those who are incorporating the cost of the first sitting of the SQE exams into their course preparation fee, or including a foundational/bridging course into their Master's–SQE for non-law graduates.

I feel that it is important to highlight the specific barriers faced by single parents – particularly those on a low income – in overcoming the financial fundamentals of a career change journey. As noted above, mothers represent the vast majority of single parents in the UK. Those that are claimants of the means-tested government benefit known as Universal Credit have outlined the barriers to career progression in a system that does not support a break in employment to complete postgraduate academic qualification. These women feel trapped in pursuing their employment status quo, even where the benefits of postgraduate study could ultimately lift them out of income support from the government entirely in the long term. This group has also clarified that any government student loan-related maintenance grant they might be able to access would not be sufficient to sustain their familial outgoings during the relevant period of study. The plight of this demographic of women is likely to warrant particular attention in any measures adopted by the legal industry to redress unjustifiable socioeconomic barriers.

Regretfully, the SRA's aspirations for broader pathways into the profession have been further confounded for mature candidates by the withdrawal of UK government funding for all graduate Level 7 apprenticeships for those aged 22 and above, which is scheduled to take place from January 2026.[17] This means that this flexible and accessible pathway to solicitor qualification is now off the table for the subject group of this chapter – a particular tragedy considering the evidence of the high rates of SQE success amongst those qualifying via this route so far.[18,19]

In respect of the regulator's intention to diversify the profession, it seems clear that a much greater injection of funding for bursaries, scholarships, and other initiatives – either from the SRA itself or from willing education and workplace training providers – will be needed to counterbalance the accessibility obstacles brought about the SQE and the removal of apprenticeship funding. In 2025, the SRA released details of its "SQE Access and

Reinvestment Fund;[20] however, as a one-off funding pot, it did not represent a substantial or sustainable resolution for those impacted by the admission changes, and greater ongoing investment will be needed going forward.

The transitionary arrangements crossfire

A specific group of graduates has been caught in something of a crossfire in the transition between the traditional and new qualification pathways, many of whom are likely to fit the late-blooming demographic by virtue of the historical dimension of the predicament. Those affected include the students that have already completed, started, paid a non-refundable deposit for, or accepted an offer of a place on the GDL or LPC before 1 September 2021.[21] The SRA provides these graduates an option to qualify under their "transitional arrangements": either via completing a formal TC, or by passing a standalone SQE2 exam alongside undergoing the two-year QWE requirement. Either of these qualification routes need to be completed before 31 December 2032, after which time these graduates would be required to complete the entire SQE.

The transitionary arrangements appear to have introduced something of a "shelf life" to the validity of LPC qualification as an admission pathway to the profession that did not exist previously. However, the more pressing issue is the fact that the SQE was not designed to be hybridized with the LPC. Consequently, pass rates for those LPC candidates taking the SQE2 as a standalone exam are significantly lower when compared to those sitting it following successful completion of the SQE1. At the time of writing, the most recent SRA annual report revealed that the majority of standalone examinees failed the exam.[22] When considered in light of the expenses associated with resitting the SQE, it seems that "unjustifiable barriers" rear up yet again for many qualification hopefuls.

Whether the theoretically broader and more flexible offering of QWE compensates for the reduction in TC opportunities since the introduction of the SQE remains to be seen, but there can be no denying that the potential of this group to qualify appears significantly narrowed. The numbers affected are not insignificant: for example, the SRA's own statistics show that, between 2011 and 2019, approximately 42 percent of LPC graduates did not progress to a TC in the data window, equating to some 4,221 students.[23]

Some SQE preparation providers have sought to bridge this gap by creating a bespoke SQE2 course for LPC graduates, which at least presents a viable pathway for affected individuals. However, given the infancy of these courses, some candidates may understandably feel compelled to complete the entire SQE syllabus at their own time and expense, despite possessing a vocational diploma that has provided an acceptable route into the profession for decades. It could have been appropriate for the regulator to inject funding into the bespoke bridging courses, given the unintended impact of the transitionary arrangements, but this seems unlikely in light of the distance it is taking from the delivery of the preparatory courses overall.

Of even greater concern is the evidence that some law firms are going beyond the regulator's stipulated arrangements by demanding SQE2 completion from the LPC graduates to whom they have *already* offered a TC (without the SQE requirement). These law firms seem to be finding it hard to manage the practicalities of training various cohorts under two different schemes, or the appear to desire the new SRA-standardized competency for their next generation of lawyers. The actions of such firms introduce hurdles that risk excluding LPC graduates from admission, going entirely against the SRA's promotion of flexibility in paths to the profession. These firms would do well to draw on the practices of those training providers that appear to be adeptly managing multiple qualification pathways concurrently.[24]

While the extent of these transitional issues has not been fully ascertained, the fallout should be urgently analyzed and addressed by the regulator and representative bodies in the profession, such as The Law Society, if fairness and diversity on the grounds of age and socioeconomic status are to be restored at the industry's point of access. For their part, law firms should bear the intentions of their regulator in mind when managing the transitionary changes and withdraw the unfair practices that are misaligned with that mission.

In the spirit of removing artificial barriers to the profession, the regulator could also consider lifting the 2032 time limit on finding a TC for transitory arrangement candidates, given what is known about the lack of TC availability. This move would not be unprecedented: the expiry date that once existed on the undergraduate law degree was lifted some years ago (which, indeed, re-opened the profession to me, as someone who qualified following a 23-year gap from the start of my LLB!).

Stage 2: The elusive breakthrough role

Completing the academic element of qualification is only half the journey for those wishing to qualify as a solicitor in England and Wales. These lawyer hopefuls must also complete a period of work-based legal training. The perennial oversupply of law graduates to available training opportunities has been well-documented. Indeed, breaking through this TC glass ceiling formed a major objective of the SRA's 2021 admission overhaul.

Qualifying work experience

In respect of the work-based element to qualification, the next generation of solicitors can now avail themselves of a broader and more flexible two-year period of QWE. QWE is described as "any experience of working in legal services which provides candidates ... with the opportunity to develop [some or all of] the competences in the Statement of Solicitor Competence".[25] While prospective solicitors must demonstrate their work-based competences to those signing off on their QWE, the regulator's position is that the SQE alone that fulfils its own assessment of competence.

QWE can be accrued cumulatively across up to four workplace settings, and the signing-off process can even be outsourced to a non-supervising solicitor who will assess the evidence of work undertaken. For candidates already work experienced in the legal arena, supervisors can sign off QWE retrospectively, provided that they are a solicitor or a compliance officer for legal practice. This has created a path into the profession for an array of career changers who operated in the wider legal arena, but who either have or would struggle to secure a TC.

Some SQE preparatory course providers are even supplying a time-limited portion of QWE as part of the course package – such as at their in-house legal advice center – thus bestowing a much-needed first point of access to the industry for those in need. For many career changers, QWE is likely to provide them with a greater degree of confidence to exit their existing careers into a more junior and less well-renumerated legal role, because these broader positions now reveal a path to qualification that was far less certain under the previous regime.

However, not everyone is embracing the new workplace learning requirements: some of the career change community has expressed fears that the super-flexible QWE requirements will not always transfer well across different legal environments on qualification (such as to private practice where experience was attained elsewhere), or be as appealing to early careers recruiters as those completing their QWE via a traditional training contract pathway. Candidates with this disposition remain focused on qualifying under the structure of a TC, and they will now find this process even more competitive in the post-SQE market.

Career changers pursuing a TC will continue to face the issues that traineeship applicants have encountered for decades: recruitment cycles with a short application window that often enlists future cohorts one or two years in advance, and multiple-stage interviews comprising lengthily application procedures, psychometric screening tests, day-long group assessment centers, and individual partner panel interviews. While these assessment processes are arguably commensurate with the gravitas and rigors of the legal profession, they are perhaps less aligned with the flexible and accessible vision of entrance to the profession advocated by the SRA. Law firms still recruiting into TC schemes for their QWE offering may need to adapt their procedures to reflect the regulator's intention that candidates are competent by virtue of passing the SQE alone.

Regardless of the considerations above, there can be no denying that the flexible dimensions to workplace qualification criteria have gone a considerable way to meeting the diversification aspirations for the legal profession at the point of entry.

The breakthrough opportunity

For those whose prior professional backgrounds are miles away from the legal sphere – as is the case for a significant proportion of career changers – that first gateway opportunity to QWE through unpaid work experience, a summer vacation scheme, a mini-pupillage, or other entry-level role remains highly elusive. A recurring obstacle appears to be the frequent requirement of a period of legal work experience for "entry-level" legal roles, which can be anything from six months to five years. Applicants are left scratching their heads as to how to crack this conundrum of "needing experience to get experience". Career changers in full-time employment and with caring responsibilities often cannot afford – both financially and logistically – to take time out to volunteer (at law clinics, support-through-court schemes, or citizens advice bureaus, for example) or complete the vacation schemes and internships that were traditionally designed to take place in line with the undergraduate term timetable.

It can be hard to maintain hope and motivation where application feedback is scarce, and career changers frequently report that they find the entire experience to be isolating and confusing. These sentiments may be particularly intensified for those mature students undertaking online study while continuing in their primary profession, where they may well lack the connections and camaraderie that their university juniors experience. In my experience, producing the volume of applications seemingly required for entry-level success proves immensely challenging for time-depleted mature women, especially those with caring responsibilities. While it can be hard to absorb relentless rejection at any stage in life, the uber-competitive nature of the legal application process leaves many mature candidates questioning to what extent they can continually absorb the sacrifices of time, money, and energy to achieve success.

A further complicating factor for vocation-changers derives from the fact that they are frequently pursuing their career pivot "in secret", not wanting to prejudice or jeopardize their current position with their employer. They are, therefore, unlikely to have the flexibility or support from their workplace to carve out time for the application process, nor will they want to be exposing their network-building efforts by creating a public professional profile on platforms like LinkedIn, which would otherwise expediate their chances of success. This cohort is likely to complete applications at night, weekends, and during annual leave, possibly around demanding senior positions in their existing careers and caring responsibilities in their personal lives. The repercussions on the personal health and wellbeing of this group are easy to comprehend: single parents, parents of children with complex needs, or those without a support network are likely be exceptionally impeded.

The issue of the renumeration on offer upon entrance to the profession also presents a real challenge to many career changers when considering their existing financial commitments and the scale of debt incurred in completing the academic stage of qualification. It is worth noting that there is no minimum salary attached to paralegal, entry-level, or even trainee solicitor roles, which can represent a financial cliff edge for those transitioning professions. If legal workplaces wish to enrich their workforce with high-quality work-and-life-experienced candidates, they will need to ensure career switch-enabling renumeration is proffered at the junior end of the scale.

Mature female candidates will need to hold their nerve as they step into the legal recruitment arena. Obtaining their proverbial "first foot on the ladder" would be greatly assisted by more robust sector-wide input: for example, legal workplaces could implement measures such as ringfencing a certain proportion of roles for female mature applicants, career changers, and those facing socioeconomic adversity.

Summary and recommendations

Entrance to the legal profession has undergone a major overhaul in recent years, and there are now seismic changes in place that open admission pathways to a far wider demographic than before, including career changers and those with a non-legal background.

The early analysis of the on-the-ground implementation of the new framework reveals that goal of removing affluence as an "unjustifiable barrier" to entrance is yet to be attained. It is likely that this obstacle will disproportionately impact mature women by virtue of their predisposition to problematic socioeconomic circumstances at this life stage. Understanding the impact of the regulatory changes on the numbers of women entering the profession will require monitoring and data analysis; to this end, the regulator will need to address the dramatic reduction in diversity data returned to it in its most recent surveys. A regular review of the exam and resit costings and the likely impact on socioeconomic diversification should be considered by those independently reviewing the SQE and addressed by the regulator accordingly. Finally, understanding the differential outcomes of the SQE by age and gender will be crucial if cross-generational female diversity at entrance to the legal profession is to be truly understood and promoted.

For their part, the legal sector businesses offering training and work experience opportunities can assist diversification efforts by emulating the competency of law firms who are successfully managing multiple training pathways into the profession. This should ideally take place without imposing supplementary requirements that are not mandated by the regulator or requiring minimum levels of work experience for entry-level roles. These legal workplaces could further promote diversity in the workforce by remaining open-minded to the transferrable skillset available from mature multi-disciplinary candidates , including those LPC candidates seeking qualification under the transitionary arrangements.

Without such proactive approaches, the current admission landscape continues to risk excluding vast swathes of highly skilled and exceptionally experienced late-blooming female talent, based on unjustifiable socioeconomic factors. This would undoubtably be a detriment to a vocation that demands the highest levels of integrity, pragmatism, and tenacity: qualities that mature women – experienced in both work and life – can offer in abundance. It is likely that bursaries, scholarships, and alternative funding pathways will need to feature heavily across all access routes, and diversity-friendly stakeholders should rise to the challenge going forward. The time for action is now.

References

1 Kurland B., "5 Ways to Thrive in Midlife", Psychology Today, 11 June 2025. See: www.psychologytoday.com/us/blog/the-well-being-toolkit/202506/5-ways-to-thrive-in-mid-life

2 Office For National Statistics, "Divorces in England and Wales: 2019 edition of this dataset". 2019. See: https://www.ons.gov.uk/peoplepopulationandcommunity/birthsdeathsandmarriages/divorce/datasets/divorcesinenglandandwales

3 Financial Conduct Authority, *Financial Lives 2024*, 16 May 2025. In: Francis-Devine B., "Household debt: statistics and impact on economy", House of Commons Library, 9 June 2025. See: https://researchbriefings.files.parliament.uk/documents/CBP-7584/CBP-7584.pdf

4 *Ibid.*

5 Diamond R., "The Motherhood Penalty in the Workplace", Psychology Today, 13 February 2023. See: https://www.psychologytoday.com/us/blog/preparing-for-parenthood/202302/the-motherhood-penalty-in-the-workplace

6 Dixon J., Ruby F., and Clery E., "Single Parents in 2023", Gingerbread, 21 March 2023. See: www.gingerbread.org.uk/our-work/policy-and-campaigns/research-publications/single-parents-in-2023/

7 The Law Society, "Annual statistics report 2022: what does the solicitor profession look like?", 7 December 2023. See: https://www.lawsociety.org.uk/topics/research/annual-statistics-report-2022

8 The Law Society, "Annual statistics report 2023", 23 January 2025. See: https://www.lawsociety.org.uk/topics/research/annual-statistics-report-2023

9 *Ibid.*

10 The Law Society, "Annual statistics report 2021", 21 September 2022. See: https://www.lawsociety.org.uk/topics/research/annual-statistics-report-2021

11 There were 197,378 solicitors on the roll as of July 2023 (see Executive Summary of "8" above), compared to 17,369 barristers. In: The Law Society, "Annual statistics report 2023", 23 January 2025. See: https://www.lawsociety.org.uk/topics/research/annual-statistics-report-2023 and Bar Standards Board, "Snapshot of the Profession – dashboard", July 2023. See: https://www.barstandardsboard.org.uk/data-and-research/snapshot-of-the-profession-dashboard.html

12 Solicitors Regulation Authority, "Solicitors Qualifying Examination (SQE) Briefing", August 2020. See: https://www.sra.org.uk/globalassets/documents/sra/news/sqe-briefing.pdf

13 *Ibid.*

14 All data and reports are available on the Solicitors Regulation Authority website at: https://sqe.sra.org.uk/exam-arrangements/sqe-reports

15 *Ibid.*

16 *Ibid.*

17 Church A. and Labib R., "UK apprenticeship funding cut to impact employers and education providers", Pinsent Masons, 6 June 2025. See: https://www.pinsentmasons.com/en-gb/out-law/news/uk-apprenticeship-funding-cut-to-impact-employers-and-education-providers

18 Solicitors Regulation Authority, "Solicitor Qualifying Examination Annual Report 2022/23". See: https://sqe.sra.org.uk/exam-arrangements/sqe-reports/sqe-annual-report-2023

19 The Solicitors Regulation Authority, "Solicitor Qualifying Examination Annual Report 2023/24". See: https://sqe.sra.org.uk/exam-arrangements/sqe-reports/sqe-annual-report-2024

20 Solicitors Regulation Authority, "SQE Access and Reinvestment Fund", 5 August 2025. See: https://www.sra.org.uk/become-solicitor/sqe/access-reinvestment-fund

21 Solicitors Regulation Authority, "SRA Authorisation of Individuals Regulations", 17 February 2025. See: https://www.sra.org.uk/solicitors/standards-regulations/authorisation-individuals-regulations

22 Solicitors Regulation Authority, "Solicitor Qualifying Examination Annual Report 2023/4". See: https://sqe.sra.org.uk/exam-arrangements/sqe-reports/sqe-annual-report-2024

23 Solicitors Regulation Authority, "Solicitors Qualifying Examination (SQE) Briefing", August 2020. See: https://www.sra.org.uk/globalassets/documents/sra/news/sqe-briefing.pdf

24 Mafuba C., "Charity talks to Jacqui Gower, Chief Operating Officer at JCP Solicitors, about the SQE Review -from an Employer's viewpoint", *Legal Women UK*, April 2025. See: https://www.legalwomen.org.uk/JacquiGower.html

25 *Ibid.*

Chapter 10:

Structuring inclusion: how women general counsel are shaping DEI through governance and procurement

By Sarah Clark, chief revenue officer, The Legal Director

"The presence of difference is not the same as the practice of inclusion."

Across the legal profession and far beyond it, the principle of access to opportunity enshrined under the banner of diversity, equity, and inclusion (DEI) has become both a uniting principle and a source of mounting disillusion. Something that, until very recently, appeared to be universally acknowledged as urgent and necessary is now being framed in certain halls of power as divisive, dispensable and – perhaps most perversely – unfair. This is playing out most visibly in the US, where the return of Donald Trump to the presidency has resulted in a major escalation in the war on DEI. The 47th president has set out to "put merit first" by issuing executive orders to "terminate every diversity, equity, and inclusion program across the entire federal government",[1] and his administration continues to very publicly pursue a punitive agenda against law firms and corporations for using race-or gender-based targets in their hiring policies.

On the other side of the Atlantic, we have not remained immune to the sea change that is currently underway in corporate America, with some UK employers now beginning to scale back their once-celebrated DEI commitments amid growing fears of a political backlash or shareholder unease. In many boardrooms, the tenor of conversations about DEI has grown much more cautious, as ambition is overtaken by wariness. Across both jurisdictions and beyond, we are seeing meaningful commitments to greater DEI gradually giving way to performative allyship and DEI greenwashing, in which appearance substitutes for action and language becomes a means of risk management, rather than progress.

The result is not simply a creeping inertia, but a widespread chilling effect. Internal teams are growing increasingly hesitant to speak uncomfortable truths; external messaging is now often crafted with plausible deniability in mind; and, although DEI is still referenced in policies and reporting frameworks, its practical weight has diminished. Where it is not structurally reinforced, DEI efforts have grown dependent on individual sponsorship or informal leadership and are thereby exposed to the risk that progress will falter if key advocates exit the organization, energy fades, or operational priorities shift.

Women – particularly women of color – are often among the first to feel the cost when DEI is deprioritized. According to LeanIn and McKinsey's *Women in the Workplace* 2023 report,[2] senior women are four times more likely than senior men to witness biased interactions in the workplace – a signal that visibility does not equate to authority and that inclusion remains fragile, even at senior levels. Women are also disproportionately tasked with sustaining cultural initiatives, modelling inclusive leadership, and absorbing the reputational consequences when progress falters. These dynamics are rarely acknowledged openly, yet they are widely recognized, not least by those repeatedly asked to lead without authority, absorb conflict without protection, or represent change without structural support. These responsibilities add to the cumulative burden placed on women in senior roles, and they sharpen the case for structural reform. The stark truth is that the work of DEI cannot rest on representation alone if it has to have any real meaning or effect. Instead, it must be embedded in how power is organized, how dissent is handled, and how standards espoused in public are applied internally under pressure.

It is the core theme of this chapter that general counsel (GC) are among the few professionals with both the visibility and authority to reinforce not only the principles – but also the practice – of DEI when its foundations are at risk. GCs sit at the point where risk and values meet, and where the stated principles of the organization are tested against the pressures of legal, commercial, and reputational complexity. Frequently having a seat at the boardroom table, we are privy to the conversations that define organizational priorities, and we are positioned within the systems – reporting, procurement, audit, compliance – that determine how decisions are made. As GCs, we are not merely observers of culture, but stewards of governance. If DEI is to make a lasting impact, it must be treated as a governance issue: something that can be scrutinized, evaluated, and enforced through structure, rather than left to cultural signaling or informal leadership.

From my own vantage point as a former GC and now chief revenue officer at a firm that places senior legal advisers, many of whom are female, into growth-focused businesses, I have seen both sides of the challenge of translating stated DEI commitments into structures that genuinely shape power and decision-making. I have observed the ways in which the language of DEI is positioned in tenders and marketing materials; how it features in recruitment metrics and public reporting; and how it relates to actual structures of influence and the everyday exercise of power. I have witnessed the influence that in-house legal leaders have as powerful strategic buyers, shaping the frameworks within which organizations are evaluated, engaged, and held to account.

This influence is becoming more visible: in 2022, women made up 67 percent of new GC appointments across Fortune 500 companies – the first year that female appointments outnumbered men in this cohort, according to a study by Russell Reynolds.[3] The same study also showed that ethnic diversity also reached a high, with 38 percent of appointees identifying as being from ethnically diverse backgrounds. While the structural barriers remain, representation at this level offers a crucial vantage point from which to press for enduring change, both within the organizations we represent and the wider commercial landscape in which we operate.

This change is urgently needed: the DEI agenda simply cannot be sustained if it remains peripheral to organizational decision-making. Instead, it must govern how influence is conferred and operationalized; therefore, it must be treated with the same seriousness and subjected to the same scrutiny that we apply to financial risk, regulatory oversight, and long-term value creation. This includes the systems we build, from governance frameworks to the technologies that determine how legal work is carried out.

Given this context, this chapter seeks to develop two interlinked arguments. The first is that, as GCs, we play a vital role within our respective organizations as senior custodians of decision-making frameworks, with the capacity to incorporate inclusive practices into the structures that define where authority and accountability reside. The second is that we also influence DEI through the decisions we make as buyers of legal services, guiding the behaviors of the firms we instruct. In both cases, the tools already exist. The question is how – and whether – we are using them.

From performance to practice: why DEI must shape how power works

Among those who argue that DEI initiatives have underdelivered, there is often a sense of frustration and a demand to see clearer, faster results. However, what is sometimes framed as a failure of principle is more often a failure of design. Too many efforts across the profession have lacked the systemic depth to gain a firm cultural foothold, focusing instead on visible outputs, such as diversity figures, recruitment pipelines, internal events, and public statements of intent.

This is not to dismiss those efforts outright; they certainly do matter. However, in the absence of mechanisms that tie DEI directly to decision-making, they become detached from the structures of influence they are supposed to challenge. Visibility may improve but, without corresponding authority, representation risks becoming symbolic. Equity is often stated as an aim; however, without governance alignment, progress stalls or reverses when priorities shift or political pressure intensifies.

This is where the role of the GC becomes critical, as we are not confined to commentary or cultural advocacy, but sit at the intersection of legal risk, governance, and commercial judgement and operate within the systems through which judgment is exercised and authority is enacted. Additionally, our remit is evolving: according to Thomson Reuters' *2025 State of the Corporate Law Department report*, GCs are placing greater emphasis on long-term value, ethical alignment, and organizational resilience as core components of departmental purpose.[4] Our vantage point within the organizations we serve thereby allows us to examine whether, rather than being merely paid lip service, DEI is, in fact, embedded into governance structures in a way that withstands scrutiny. That includes how decisions are made; whose perspectives are given weight; and whether internal mechanisms are designed to uphold DEI when conditions become more complex.

These dynamics are not always visible in formal reporting, but they are well-understood by those navigating them day-to-day. They manifest in how feedback is handled; whose objections are absorbed or sidelined; and whether dissenting voices are treated as inconvenient or instructive. For those navigating these dynamics – particularly women and others historically excluded from senior roles – the absence of structural support increases the risk of isolation, reputational exposure, and stalled progression. The demands of visibility are rarely matched by an equivalent share of influence. In practice, the cost of these systemic gaps is frequently borne disproportionately by women, especially those from under-represented backgrounds. They are often placed in roles that convey profile, but confer limited influence. They may be expected to provide presence, reassurance, or cultural insight, yet remain excluded from the decisions that follow.

Although rarely addressed explicitly, the realities these patterns reflect are all too familiar to many women, and backed up by the data: although we have certainly seen much progress in terms of female representation within the profession over recent decades, with the International Bar Association estimating that women now make up nearly half the legal profession globally, only 38 percent hold senior leadership roles.[5] This underscores a wider truth: inclusion that is not reinforced by formal structures will tend to depend on informal sponsorship, personal goodwill, or situational discretion, which are conditions that are inherently variable and cannot be relied upon in the long term.

For women in senior in-house legal roles, these dynamics also come into sharp relief. We are often expected to model inclusive behaviors, act as informal mentors, and absorb cultural labor that is rarely acknowledged, let alone rewarded. However, our position also affords us a distinct vantage point. We are close enough to see where systems fall short, and senior enough to question whether inclusion is genuinely being integrated within the processes that determine who is heard, who is protected, and who can raise concerns without being sanctioned, officially or otherwise.

The distinction between activity and impact discussed here plays out in the architecture of internal governance. If DEI is absent from board reporting, risk dashboards, audit trails, or post-incident reviews, its presence in messaging or cultural initiatives cannot be relied on. GCs are well-placed to interrogate these realities because we operate across functions, engage directly with senior decision-makers, and are trained to evaluate organizational resilience in legal, ethical, structural, and reputational terms. This responsibility includes asking whether DEI has been systemically enabled to endure in our organization as a standard of practice so deeply embedded that it remains intact when conditions become complex or politically exposed.

Designing for dissent: how governance enables DEI under stress

DEI is often described in terms of belonging, support, and psychological safety. These are important and necessary conditions for participation, but inclusion also depends on an organization's capacity to absorb criticism: to hear what it does not want to hear; confront discomfort without defaulting to defensiveness; and allow disagreement to influence outcomes. The ability to do so is as much a matter of organizational design as it is of culture in its broadest sense. As touched on above, it is in moments of reputational risk, commercial urgency, or internal disagreement that these structures are tested. In those moments, it is not the stated values that determine the outcome so much as the habits, hierarchies, and reporting lines through which those values are expected to be operationalized.

An example offered by Jordan Breslow,[6] former GC at the software company Opsware, helps to illustrate the point. In the early 2000s, during a period of significant market volatility, the company considered a common but ethically questionable method of valuing stock options for new employees. The proposed approach – which involved pricing options according to the lowest market value over a preceding period, rather than on the date of issue – had become widespread. On the surface, it seemed financially rational. However, after reviewing the regulatory implications and seeking external advice, Breslow advised against it. The CEO accepted his recommendation, later crediting Breslow with keeping him out of jail, and the company avoided the kind of scrutiny that would go on to have a highly detrimental impact on others in the sector.

What enabled Breslow's intervention was not merely sound judgment on his part, but also the organizational structure within which he operated. Breslow reported directly to the CEO and operated in an environment in which constructive criticism was expected, rather than penalized. His authority to dissent was not contingent on his own boldness or political capital; it was designed into the GC's role. This is the crucial point. Ethical scrutiny, cultural challenge, and principled resistance must be structurally supported, instead of personally improvised.

In many organizations, that support is inconsistent. Female GCs and other senior legal leaders, particularly those from under-represented groups, are frequently expected to shoulder a disproportionate share of cultural responsibility. We may be relied upon to mediate tensions, advise on sensitive issues, or act as default representatives on matters of inclusion, often without formal remit or recognition. These responsibilities are rarely captured in role descriptions or performance assessments, but they exert a cumulative weight. For those among us whose identities diverge from the dominant norms of leadership – whether through race, social background, disability, or neurodivergence – that weight is magnified by the pressure we feel to maintain credibility while navigating environments in which we may be perceived as exceptions, rather than the norm.

From a governance perspective, this is not simply inequitable, but also a sign of institutional immaturity. A system that claims to value DEI but fails to formally recognize the labor that sustains it cannot credibly claim to be embedding it. In other words, the presence of difference is not the same as the practice of inclusion. Representation may satisfy visual expectations, but unless that presence is matched by structural authority – the ability to dissent, to lead, to steer decisions – it remains symbolic. This is why reporting lines matter: where GCs report, and to whom we are accountable, sends a clear signal about the organization's willingness to invite scrutiny. A system in which the GC reports only to the executive may offer operational proximity, but it does not necessarily provide the independence we require to voice objections regarding behavior or culture at the highest level. A structure that enables or expects us to simultaneously report to the chair of the board communicates something different: a recognition that consistency of principle is integral to good governance.

This distinction is more than procedural. It determines whether DEI can be enacted under pressure or whether, in the absence of systemic reinforcement, it is allowed to dissipate. Organizations that conflate constructive criticism with disruption may interpret challenge as disloyalty, even when it is intended to protect long-term value. However, dissent, when channeled through trusted frameworks, is a signal of integrity, rather than disorder. If we as GCs are penalized – whether explicitly or tacitly – for raising cultural concerns, those around us will begin to self-censor long before those concerns surface through formal channels.

In summary, if DEI is to be treated as a matter of governance, rather than reputation, GCs must then be positioned accordingly. Our ability to ask uncomfortable questions – about who is trusted, who is heard, and how decisions are made – cannot rely on force of personality or informal access. It requires us to have formal standing and independent reporting lines, and to operate within a professional culture that treats our scrutiny as a form of institutional care: a commitment to standards, accountability and long-term coherence.

General counsel as strategic buyers: shaping the legal supply chain

Our influence as GC extends beyond the internal workings of the organization and into the legal market more broadly. Through procurement, panel appointments, and matter reviews, we help to define the expectations that law firms internalize and the behaviors they reward. For many, this influence is clearest during request for proposal (RFP) processes, when firms are required to demonstrate alignment with client values, extending beyond pure legal competence to include culture, collaboration, and DEI.

However, the gap between presentation and practice is often wide. Many GCs speak candidly about the mismatch between what is presented in tenders and what is experienced in delivery. Diverse pitch teams give way to homogenous core teams. Lawyers from under-represented groups are brought to the fore in RFP processes, and then subtly excluded once significant or strategically sensitive work begins. It is a pattern familiar across firms – and one that women GCs, particularly those from historically excluded backgrounds, are acutely attuned to.

This misalignment between what gets promised and what is actually delivered is well-documented. For example, a 2024 survey conducted by Leopard Solutions in collaboration with Above the Law gathered responses from 643 attorneys from under-represented groups at top US law firms.[7,8] Nearly one third (32percent) said that they had been invited to client pitches, but were excluded from the actual work; in 85 percent of those cases, the work fell squarely within their area of expertise. One response captures the experience with disarming clarity:

> *"Happens all the time. The client has diversity requirements... they want a Black person in the meeting to secure the work. The work comes in, I don't know about it, and it goes elsewhere, usually to a non-diverse person."*

The result is a dynamic in which DEI is acknowledged rhetorically but seldom examined in substance, a sign that it too often functions as a brand signal, rather than an operational priority. We cannot afford for DEI simply to be treated as a marketing asset in this way; it must be more deeply integrated into the way work is structured, shared, and rewarded. For those of us working in-house, that requires moving beyond rhetorical alignment and focusing instead on behavioral consistency. As GCs, we need to ask how firms behave under pressure, how they formalize decision-making, and whether individuals from under-represented backgrounds feel equipped to contribute, critique, and be heard throughout the lifecycle of the engagement.

Some of us are already doing this – up to a point. According to the Association of Corporate Counsel's 2022 DE&I Survey,[9] only 38 percent of GCs said that they had asked firms to track diversity metrics or make DEI-related commitments. Of these, only 7 percent said that they were doing so in any structured or advanced way, suggesting that, even among motivated clients, formal accountability remains rare. The result is evident in the overall rating:

when asked to score their firms' progress in delivering diverse legal teams, GCs gave an average of just 5.9 out of 10. The message this sends is subtle but clear: even when DEI is raised at the point of selection, it is seldom reinforced in delivery. Unless we, as clients, are willing to revisit, reward, and require inclusive behavior throughout the engagement, firms are unlikely to treat it as a substantive operational priority.

Part of the challenge is practical, with many GCs lacking consistent mechanisms for assessing how firms actually behave in practice. This is where frameworks like the Law Firm Maturity Index (LFMI) can provide useful clarity.[10] Developed by the Maturity Institute, the index assesses organizational health across indicators such as human value realization, purpose alignment, and cultural resilience. The results are telling: while most firms espouse inclusive values, few demonstrate the kind of organizational maturity required to deliver on them, with no firm scoring above a B in the most recent LFMI ranking at the time of writing (July 2025).[11] When we embed these expectations into tenders and panel reviews, we send a clear signal: the language law firms use to express their commitments is of much less interest and importance than the question of whether those commitments are demonstrably reinforced by robust infrastructure, behavior, and oversight.

The same principle applies to the O-Shaped Request for Legal Services toolkit, a framework developed by in-house leaders to align procurement criteria with the behaviors that sustain inclusive, high-performing teams.[12] The toolkit equips GCs with practical, consistent language to assess the cultural dimensions of legal service delivery – from how work is delegated and credited to how psychological safety is maintained under pressure. The mechanism is clear: what clients ask, revisit, and reward is what law firms will prioritize.

This collective approach is a powerful one. As GCs, it is tempting to regard our role as a solitary one, each of us striving in isolation to make better decisions. However, real change is more likely when our expectations are shared. When in-house leaders begin asking the same questions – and rewarding the firms that answer them meaningfully – the market responds. This is the value of shared frameworks: they reduce ambiguity; bring where responsibility resides into sharper focus; and create momentum. While no single client can reshape the profession, GCs can certainly set a higher bar together.

The cumulative power we wield as GCs extends to the adoption of legal technology, particularly with regard to artificial intelligence (AI). As legal tech grows more sophisticated and integrated in day-to-day practice, the decisions we make collectively about which tools to procure, and on what terms, become increasingly consequential. AI, in particular, presents both promise and risk in this context. It has the potential to widen access to legal knowledge and reduce inefficiency, but it can also replicate bias, obscure accountability, and centralize control in ways that disadvantage those who are already under-represented. This is why DEI must be treated as a fundamental design principle of the technology itself, rather than an afterthought or secondary consideration. As GCs, our position at the intersection of ethics, risk, and innovation enables us to ask the questions others may overlook. Who trained this model, and on what data? What assumptions are being encoded? How is bias being tested, and whose responsibility is to make changes if it is found? Is this tool explainable, and does it accommodate different ways of working? These are not abstract concerns; they cut to the heart of whether technology serves inclusion or undermines the very principles of DEI. Just as we evaluate law firms on culture and conduct as well as outcomes, so too must we scrutinize the systems that support our work. This means collaborating with HR and IT functions to establish robust AI governance frameworks that encompass explainability, auditability, and inclusion. It also means championing mechanisms that expand, rather than constrain, who gets to participate in legal work: tools that challenge legacy hierarchies, rather than reinforce them.

Against this backdrop, the critical question is whether we are actively using the mechanisms available to us to embed DEI principles in practice, rather than simply endorsing them in theory. What GCs reward, revisit, and require governs what others prioritize. The means to achieve this already exist – they simply need to be used with more rigor and greater intent. To that end, Boxes 1 and 2 contain a non-exhaustive framework of levers that GCs can pull internally and externally to reinforce system-wide inclusion and shape DEI-enhancing behaviors across the legal supply chain.

Box 1: Internal behaviors to operationalize DEI

- Ensure that DEI is referenced explicitly in board-level reporting and risk dashboards.
- Build inclusion into audit, governance and escalation structures – not just policy.
- Interrogate team structures: who holds influence, who is protected, who is heard?

- Create feedback systems that capture not just outcomes, but how decisions were experienced.
- Recognize and reward cultural contribution in performance and promotion frameworks.

Box 2: External behaviors to operationalize DEI

- Ask firms how they behave under pressure, not just what values they endorse.
- Use tools like the Law Firm Maturity Index and O-Shaped evaluation criteria.
- Assess how inclusion is maintained during delivery, not just signaled at the outset.
- Reward firms that demonstrate consistency, psychological safety, and inclusive delegation.
- Treat AI as a governance issue: ask vendors to evidence inclusion in design and impact.

Conclusions

If this chapter has argued anything, it is that DEI will not endure unless it is systemically enabled. It cannot rest on surface commitments – statements of intent, symbolic gestures, or performative visibility – but must be made an integral component of the architecture of power: how it is distributed, examined, and held to account. In this context, DEI must be designed into the frameworks that govern how organizations operate and should be reinforced structurally when conditions become difficult. Whether in corporations, public institutions, or professional service firms, when DEI is invoked but its foundations are ignored, organizations do more than fall short of their ideals: they weaken the credibility of the very work they claim to support.

This is not a counsel of despair, nor a plea for louder advocacy. It is an invitation to approach DEI as a matter of professional standards; as something that shapes how decisions are made and how accountability is maintained, not merely how the organization presents itself externally. As women in-house leaders, we see these tensions from multiple vantage points. We have learned to read between the lines of what firms say and what they actually deliver. We also see, from inside our organizations, where internal governance reinforces inclusive practice, and where it allows cultural risk to accumulate unexamined. This is where our responsibilities are matched by real influence: we are close enough to the relevant systems to understand how they function, and senior enough to determine how they evolve. Through both governance and procurement, we help to define the conditions under which organizational principles are upheld in moments of clarity and consensus, as well as during periods of stress, change, or reputational pressure. In both domains, we have the opportunity to ask whether commitments are being honored through formalized structures, behavior, and oversight, rather than being merely reflected in outward messaging. The levers available to us are already clear – what matters now is how deliberately and consistently we apply them.

The legal profession has never lacked for language. However, at a time when DEI is being contested politically, legally, and reputationally, the deeper test lies in how we are empowered to act to defend and preserve it, rather than in the words we choose to discuss it. If DEI is to withstand the forces that currently assail it, we – as its champions – cannot depend on our individual convictions or personal influence alone. We require the assistance of robust systems: reporting lines, evaluation processes, feedback mechanisms, and behavioral standards that hold firm across time and context. Rather than stifling dissent, these systems must absorb it constructively and should understand governance not as the enemy of culture, but as its most credible expression. If the profession wishes to retain its claim to principled leadership within the world of commerce, as well as in public life, it must be prepared to demonstrate that its commitment to inclusion can withstand scrutiny: deliberately, structurally, and with the long term in view.

References

1 The White House, "Fact Sheet: President Donald J. Trump Removes DEI From the Foreign Service", 18 March 2025. See: https://www.whitehouse.gov/fact-sheets/2025/03/fact-sheet-president-donald-j-trump-removes-dei-from-the-foreign-service

2 Field E., Krivkovich A., Kügele S., Robinson N., and Yee L., *Women in the Workplace 2023*, McKinsey & Company, 5 October 2023. See: https://www.mckinsey.com/featured-insights/diversity-and-inclusion/women-in-the-workplace-2023

3 Dow C., "More Inclusive Leadership, More Experience: Meet the Fortune 500 General Counsels", Russell Reynolds, 21 March 2023. See: https://www.russellreynolds.com/en/insights/reports-surveys/more-inclusive-leadership-more-experience-meet-the-fortune-500-general-counsels

4 Abbott M., Duffy E., Josten W., Leach L, and Seemer S., 2025 *State of the Corporate Law Department report*, Thomson Reuters Institute, 2025. See:

https://legalsolutions.thomsonreuters.co.uk/content/dam/ewp-m/documents/legal/en/pdf/reports/2025-state-of-corporate-law-department-report

5 International Bar Association Legal Policy & Research Unit, *50:50 by 2030: A longitudinal study into gender disparity in law*, 2024. See: https://www.ibanet.org/document?id=IBA-Gender-Progress-Report-2024

6 White B., "Jordan Breslow: Former General Counsel Whose Advice Stopped His CEO Going To Jail", The Crafty Show, 4 April 2023, See: https://craftycounsel.co.uk/podcasts/jordan-breslow-former-general-counsel-whose-advice-stopped-his-ceo-going-to-jail

7 Leopard Solutions, *Diversity in Big Law: Insights and Strategies from the Perspectives of the Underrepresented Attorneys*, 2024. See: https://www.leopardsolutions.com/thought-leadership/Diversity-in-law-2024

8 Leopard Solutions and Above The Law, "Unseen: Diverse Attorneys Detail Imbalances In Biglaw", Above The Law, 17 May 2024. See: https://abovethelaw.com/2024/05/unseen-diverse-attorneys-detail-imbalances-in-biglaw

9 Association of Corporate Counsel, *General Counsel: Diversity, Equity & Inclusion Survey*, 2022. See: https://www.acc.com/sites/default/files/2023-01/ACC_GC_DE%26I_Report.pdf

10 LexSolutions, "The Law Firm Maturity Index (LFMI)", 2025. See: https://lexsolutions.com/law-firm-maturity-index-lfmi

11 Woollard S. and Kanwar M., *Law Firm Maturity Index 2024 Rankings: Inaugural Report*, 30 October 2024. See: http://www.hrmaturity.com/wp-content/uploads/2024/11/LFMI-Ranking-Report-3.pdf

12 O Shaped, "The O Shaped RFP Toolkit", 2025. See: https://oshaped.com/rfp

Chapter 11: Your own potential, your own terms: crafting your career through consultancy

By Rachel Brushfield, founder, EnergiseLegal

This chapter will explore the ways in which consultancy can enable women lawyers to sidestep the systemic barriers still inherent in private practice, especially traditional law firms. It includes data about the consultant lawyer market; the journeys of women lawyers at different levels of seniority in private practice in the UK; and the ways in which being a consultant lawyer empowers women lawyers, especially those with caregiving responsibilities, to craft a work–life blend that works for them and receive higher earnings for their effort. Downsides of being a consultant lawyer are also shared. Quotes from female founders of platform law firms and female consultant lawyers who are mothers provide insights "from the horse's mouth".

The necessity to plan ahead, establish a personal brand, and build your career capital is examined for those interested in being a consultant lawyer, taking into consideration with more competition and with the platform law firm market maturing and changing in shape.

The useful role of consultant lawyer work as a component of a portfolio career providing financial certainty, is discussed. Portfolio careers are a growing trend in the changing world of work, with client work being combined with other legal or non-legal work components. Contrasting examples of women lawyer portfolio careerists and their different work mixes bring this concept to life. Action planning concludes the chapter, enabling you to turn insights into actions.

The consultant lawyer market: market size and trends

The consultant lawyer market is continuing to grow. Codex Edge's 2025 *Platform Firms Report* provides useful data and analysis.[1] The market is maturing, becoming more competitive for platform firms and consultant lawyers alike. Consolidation is likely to happen, as is increased specialization, with niche firms becoming more commonly established. In 2024, twice as many lawyers opted to join platform law firms rather than enter traditional legal practice.

Different firms have varying focuses, hiring strategies, and propositions, and continue to be robust in attracting talent. Firms with a compelling proposition that prioritize the experience of consultant lawyers in terms of support are likely to experience sustained success. Most of the consultant lawyers recruited by platform firms have between eight and 18 years of post-qualification experience (PQE), with a good client following and well-established business development and client relationship management skills.

However, as time goes on, it is likely that younger or less experienced solicitors will be interested in becoming a consultant lawyer. Focusing on developing their networking abilities, creating a compelling personal brand, and building marketing and business development skills early on in their career will help them to achieve their ambitions. For early-career women solicitors considering whether to start a family or with other caregiving responsibilities, thinking ahead to which roles in the legal profession are compatible with caregiving and their own career aspirations is wise. Much has been written about how younger cohorts of lawyers, especially millennials and Gen Z, seek travel opportunities and are interested in early responsibility in their career. Becoming a consultant lawyer can present a good component of a portfolio career for them, around which other components can be built.

Sex or gender demographics currently are not measured for the consultant lawyer market. The percentage of consultant lawyers who are women is estimated to be between 60 to 65 percent. More women are moving to consultancy because of the flexibility and family-friendly nature of the role, which can help them to achieve a healthier work–life blend than is commonly possible in private practice. For example, at Setfords, a UK Top 100-ranked platform law firm, 63 percent of consultant lawyers are women.[2]

The Modern Family Index UK *Legal Sector Report 2025* shares data about lawyer parents specifically, and the challenges that they face compared with other professionals. According to this report, 71 percent of legal sector parents had "childcare breakdowns" (i.e., problems with prearranged childcare that clashed with their work) in the last 12 months.[3] Some 77 percent reported carefully considering their childcare options before accepting a promotion or a new job, as this is such an important factor in creating ease and avoiding stress.[4] Some 36 percent of legal sector parents report high stress levels, and 74 percent have concerns about the mental health of their children.[5] Flexibility tops the list of what matters when it comes to work for legal sector parents. Indeed, the desire to have flexibility in working patterns is a clear theme, both in terms of days in the office and in working hours. For many reasons, as a working parent, the ability to choose your own hours is a massive advantage, and the return to the office mandated by hybrid working can be a challenge.

Private practice, women, and seniority: the data

Some 53 percent of all lawyers in the UK in 2025 are women, according to the Solicitors Regulation Authority (SRA). Women represent 47 percent of salaried partners; 60 percent of junior lawyers or newly qualified solicitors; and approximately 41 percent of junior barristers. However, significantly fewer women than men are full-equity partners: 32 percent.[6] This is also the case at the most senior barrister ranks. This could be due to the fact that, in the majority of heterosexual partnerships, women remain responsible for a disproportionate amount of childcare and household management. The woman is usually the first person to be called if there be a problem with childcare or at school, or if a child becomes ill during the working week. One of my clients – who successfully negotiated a four-day week in a head of legal role to enable flexibility, as her partner often works abroad – calls this being the "CEO of the household". Combining parenthood with a busy full-time lawyering job is a challenge, and many working mothers choose to work part-time to create some breathing room.

Women's partnership rates vary considerably by firm size. In larger firms with over 50 partners, only 28 percent of full-equity partners and 41 percent of salaried partners are women. In mid-size firms with ten to 50 partners, 47 percent of salaried partners and 31 percent of full-equity partners are women. In small firms with six to nine partners, the proportion of women partners is higher than average at 52 percent. In very small firms with two to five partners, 24 percent of full-equity partners are women. In single-partner firms, 37 percent of partners are women.

Consultancy: the way forward for women lawyers?

In private practice, when women desiring to have children step off the career ladder to do so, this is often at a time in their careers when their employer is beginning to recoup the investment made in their training and mentoring. While maternity leave and pay is essential, many firms still perceive this as a cost, either consciously or unconsciously.

Additionally, when attending a conference, I was once informed by employees at a Magic Circle firm that many of their women lawyers were leaving the firm soon after they returned from maternity leave, despite the fact that they had received returner coaching support. Analysis of the issue indicated that women were expected to hit the ground running upon their return to work from maternity leave. The conscious and unconscious demand from their employer was to deliver 100 percent of fee-earning targets from their first day back, which was simply unrealistic at such a major period of transition. The pressure that they were under – just after having a new member of their family – was too great to bear for many, understandably. From coaching women, I have noticed that it is common for their values and what is important to them to change when having children.

Despite firms introducing paternity leave options, very few fathers take this up, so the lion's share of domestic labor falls to the mother. Women tend to perform a disproportionate amount of childcare and household management when compared to men in a heterosexual partnership. Women, therefore, lack time to network and engage in business development, especially outside of conventional working hours, such as mornings and evenings. When going back to work, women often put their head down and focus on what needs to be done, missing the opportunity to promote themselves to stakeholders in the firm.

These obstacles to women's success are not only limited to the penalization of working mothers, but manifest in systemic prejudices, such as delegation bias. In the legal profession, this shows up as women performing behind-the-scenes work while men gain visibility and accolades through client-facing work in deals and cases, especially high-profile ones.

Choosing to become a consultant lawyer may present a means for women to side-step many of the systemic barriers to success that are still prevalent in private practice, especially in the more traditional parts of the profession. The benefits of being a consultant lawyer are magnified for working mothers or those with caregiving or other demanding responsibilities outside of work. Consultant lawyers can set their own schedules, allowing them to work when it suits them and their clients. This flexibility is especially valuable for women balancing professional and personal commitments, such as family responsibilities or childcare, without the constraints of a rigid 9–5 schedule. The ability to work remotely and avoid commuting enables women lawyers to better integrate their professional and personal lives, attend family events, or manage other priorities without sacrificing their careers. Additionally, the move to home-working, remote meetings, and online networking on platforms such as LinkedIn has helped working women needing flexibility in terms of time and location.

Additionally, consultant roles often eliminate the pressure of traditional law firm hierarchies and partnership tracks, providing a more empowering environment for women to progress on their own terms. Women can avoid the presenteeism and occasionally toxic and competitive cultures still prevalent in some firm while maintaining control over the type of work they take on, the clients they serve, and how they develop their practice. This autonomy supports career growth and allows women to focus on areas that align with their expertise and interests. Greater control over workload and schedule can lead to improved health and wellbeing, reducing stress and allowing time for self-care.

Choosing to become a consultant lawyer, rather than setting up one's own firm, means peace of mind in terms of support with compliance, governance, and professional indemnity insurance and any necessary tools or platforms. Many consultant models allow lawyers to retain a significantly larger share of their billings – often up to 70–80 percent – compared to the traditional firm structure, where lawyers might keep only a third of their billings. This can lead to substantially higher income for the same or less work. In addition, many platform firms offer a referral fee for work passed on to other consultant lawyers within their network. They also gain a collaborative community or 'tribe' to network with and support. In addition, they receive more money for the time and effort that they put in, compared with private practice, which is motivating and in addition get a referral fee for referring work to other consultant lawyers in the firm.

Overall, the consultant model offers women lawyers – especially those with caregiving responsibilities – a pathway to greater financial reward, autonomy, and flexibility, making it an increasingly attractive alternative to traditional legal careers. As part of writing this chapter, I asked Philip Lewis, founder of Philip Lewis Professional Services, for his view. As someone who knows the consultant lawyer market well and understands the perspectives of both consultant lawyers and platform law firms, Philip commented:

> *"My job is to facilitate introductions between aspiring consultant lawyers and platform law firms to enable a good cultural fit and alignment between both. As a natural prolific and proactive networker, I act as a talent scout and connector on the ground in London. The consultant lawyer model provides many benefits, especially for women lawyers [who are] working mothers, who [...] often do the majority of childcare and household management. Lack of time, not talent, can affect their career prospects and*

advancement through the ranks in private practice. Being able to choose your own working patterns, enjoy flexibility, be your own boss, be part of a group of like-minded consultants, and earn more for the effort that you put in as a consultant lawyer makes sense!

My advice to young solicitors aspiring to become a consultant lawyer in future would be that it is never too early to develop your business development efforts, networking skills, and marketing competence and confidence. This – combined with a network of introducers – will help you to build a client following, enabling you to become an attractive proposition to your target platform firm."

Carly Jermyn, founder of Woodstock Legal Services, which was deemed one of the top firms with fewer than 30 consultants in Codex Edge's 2025 *Platform Firms Report*, had this to say:

"For me, consultancy opens the door for women to take greater control of their careers in what is still a very male top-heavy profession. However, the big shift I've seen over the last couple of years is men choosing consultancy, because it allows them to better support their female partners (wives, mothers of their children) to pursue their career. This is real progress in my eyes."

Insights from women consultant lawyers

In November 2024, EnergiseLegal conducted qualitative research with a range of women consultant lawyers with different legal specialisms who are currently working at various platform law firms. These are their views on becoming and being a consultant lawyer, expressed in their own words.

"I'd considered the idea of consultancy for some considerable time; through coaching, I made the decision to go for it."

"I had considered setting up my own law firm, but [I] looked into the regulatory side and decided I wanted some back-office support for the admin!"

"70 percent is a lot more than the 25–35 percent I was getting [in terms of] fees, with the added benefit that I don't have to deal with regulatory stuff, and have business development support to hand, as well."

"I feel so much better in myself not being weighed down by a poor working environment – I'm creating my own, and although I'm responsible for my working environment, my work/life balance, [and] my income, I don't feel a weight of that because I'm doing things I want to do in a way I want to do them."

"I have observed that the kind of people who become a consultant lawyer are 40+, [with] 15+ years' PQE, usually with families, or who want flexibility and independence – a lot of women who've grown disillusioned with traditional law firms."

"Think carefully before making the leap: build your personal brand and personal contacts and referrers; plan carefully; make sure you've got enough money in case you don't immediately start earning (platforms can take a while to pay and some practice areas only bill on completion, so you could be waiting months for a transaction to complete); [and] speak to people who've 'been there, done it'. Be aware of the support you have in a law firm (team to delegate to; personal assistant; in-house business development) and check you're happy to operate much more independently."

"I was struggling to find a sustainable rhythm working in traditional practice – [between] targets, KPIs, billable hours, [and] fee generation – that allowed me to still deliver on and fulfil my career goals and ambitions [in] working towards partnership, but still be 'present' and visible at home to a young family. Having greater autonomy about the types of clients I worked with, the type of work I did, what value I could provide to those clients, and whilst having greater flexibility around my own work/life balance has been invaluable."

"I feel the old, more 'traditional' model in law and slaving to billable hours is quite outdated in 2024."

"I had already started to build up my own client following and practice. However, I was a little concerned that this was 'still growing', having come back from maternity leave not too long ago. Whilst the work and pipeline have been growing, the consultancy model has allowed me to look at other skills I held and where I could deploy into other areas that complement my practice, and start developing a portfolio career."

"What appealed to me about becoming a consultant lawyer was autonomy and flexibility; reaping a direct reward for my efforts; a sense of empowerment with my career being in my hands; no need to 'climb the greasy pole'; no bureaucracy and politics; and the ability to focus wholly on clients and set my own rates."

"To succeed as a consultant lawyer, you need to be proactive, flexible, have a drive to succeed, the ability to back yourself, able to spot and capitalize on new opportunities, be consistent in work quality, and provide excellent client service."

"Being a consultant lawyer is an attractive model for women with young children looking for flexibility, older lawyers looking to wind down, [and], increasingly, younger lawyers looking for freedom and the ability to reap direct rewards from their efforts and run their own business. It works well for employment lawyers, due to the regular nature of the work, and for property lawyers, due to the insurance cost of setting up alone and the regular/standalone nature of the work."

"You have to rely on yourself, so build your own reputation."

"Platform law firms want lawyers who are collegiate and willing to develop their network – self-starters who wants to work independently and who are motivated. Traditional law firms need to adapt so that they prevent talent drain. Talent is their competitive advantage. With the unknown impact of AI on the legal profession, this is a high priority not to be neglected. The challenge for law firms is having the headspace to tackle these issues with fee-earning targets."

"I have noticed that more and more lawyers are leaving traditional firms for the consultancy model. Clients are more flexible and willing to engage with such firms."

"I wish I had become a consultant lawyer sooner!"

The drawbacks of being a consultant lawyer

Being a consultant lawyer does have its drawbacks. While consultancy can offer autonomy and flexibility, lawyers can face financial insecurity, lack of institutional support, challenges in accessing high-quality work, and persistent biases, all of which can complicate career sustainability and advancement in this role.

Consultant lawyers typically lose the security of a regular monthly salary and associated benefits, such as maternity leave and sick pay, which are often provided by firms. This can be a significant concern for women, especially those balancing family responsibilities. An absence of employer maternity pay means that this must be self-funded and carefully planned for, which is not an inconsiderable feat. Additionally, self-employment means that there is always worry about where the next fees will come from. This financial unpredictability can be stressful and may disproportionately impact women, who often face additional caregiving duties that may undermine their ability to engage in business development. While consultancy can offer flexibility, it also demands self-management and client acquisition efforts that may increase workload and financial unpredictability.

Women lawyers often struggle to find mentors and sponsors, particularly male allies, within traditional firms. As consultants, they may face even greater isolation and less access to informal networks that facilitate career advancement and business development. However, this varies greatly between the different platform law firms.

As consultants, women may have to work harder to establish their reputation without the backing of a firm's brand, which can be a barrier to attracting clients and gaining recognition. It is common for solicitors to feel uncomfortable being the "face" of their own brand, especially with the growing importance of social media. Having the backing of a firm's brand – not your own – is more comfortable for some, especially introverts, so personal development to explore limiting beliefs about this is useful, as beliefs drive behavior. I have spoken at more events aimed at helping women to overcome blocks about marketing themselves, for both lawyers and non-lawyers alike, than for any other topic. I have found that women – who often experience "imposter syndrome" – and lawyers specifically – who are trained to see the risks in everything – perceive "blowing their own trumpet" as boastful and pushy. Identifying a comfortable strategy and approach to market yourself in a way that works for you creates ease, reduces anxiety, and increases results. Indirect approaches often work well, especially for introverts. Indirect approaches include thought leadership (such as writing articles), client case studies, client testimonials, awards, inclusion in the Legal 500 and Chambers and Partners' league tables, and so on.

The importance of building your career capital, personal branding, and client following

To become a consultant lawyer, it is especially important to have good career capital – ie, what makes you marketable – and a robust client following. In particular, a client following makes you appealing to platform law firms. Each firm has their own recruitment policy, but having a client following is a must-have for the vast majority. To achieve this requires planning, time, and thought. It doesn't happen overnight; it is the result of creating and executing a strategy.

Having loyal clients with whom you have a strong relationship, who provide you with repeat business, and who are willing to recommend you to others is an asset. Lawyers with robust client followings can deliver immediate income streams and demonstrate their ability to generate business independently. This can be achieved by going the extra mile with your clients, establishing excellent verbal and written communication. Trust, rapport, being competent and skilled, and connecting with people via good emotional intelligence all helps you to build a good client following. Being proactive and supporting your clients to be successful in their own careers is important. Cultivating a following requires continual investment, so expect to put in time and effort.

Career capital is multi-faceted. Thought leadership, manifested in the writing of books, chapters, articles, blogs, or guest blogs and recording videos or podcasts, is a critical component. Keynote speeches, such as Ted Talks, and qualifications, such as an MBA, MA, or PhD or specialist accreditations, build your legal niche and help you become the "go-to" lawyer for your area of expertise, differentiating you from your competitors. Speaking two or more languages can also be a real asset in attracting clients and securing a position as a consultant lawyer with your preferred platform law firm. Additionally, who is in your network – or not – on platforms such as LinkedIn says something about you.

A distinctive personal brand sets you apart, which is useful in the digital age. An easy-to-remember 3-word description of yourself and your services can be beneficial: it positions you clearly, is immediately visible on platforms like LinkedIn, and helps you to be remembered and gain word-of-mouth referrals. If you can trademark it – even better. Richard Hiron's The Hironator™, Chrissie Lightfoot's The Naked Lawyer and The Entrepreneur Lawyer, and Nick Freeman's Mr Loop Hole™ are three examples of lawyers with distinctive personal brands.

You need to be confident and competent at marketing yourself and engaging in business development. Some platform firms, such as Bamboo Law, provide their consultant lawyers with support with marketing, networking, social media, and business development. Creating a new business plan, stretch goals, and updated SMART (specific, measurable, achievable, relevant, and time-bound) career capital goals annually will help you to build your marketability and create sustainable success. To assess your marketability, you can measure and track your personal brand using AI. Asking Perplexity AI "What does [your name] specialize in?" will summarize all available information about you and your business online. This can help you to set new career capital goals and decide what marketing and business development will build or pivot your brand territory. Microsoft Copilot can also do this.

Building a portfolio career

A portfolio career comprises multiple streams of work and income, and represents a future-proof occupational track, as you are not putting all your eggs in one basket. Components of a portfolio career vary greatly and can include one or more paid or unpaid part-time roles, such as non-executive directorships, freelance lawyering, volunteering, part-time judicial work, and so on. The mix can be adjusted as your life, needs, or professional context change, such as having children, becoming an "empty nester", or shifts in the external market and client needs. Portfolio careers are also popular with pre-retirees who want a gentle slope, rather than a steep drop, towards retirement, such as experienced partners who want to continue working in a more flexible way and on their own terms. With an ageing population and longer working lives, taking career breaks to travel, pursue personal interests, and study will become increasingly common. In particular, a sabbatical to study and gain a higher qualification/accreditation can build your career capital, which is important when considering the growing competition in the platform law firm market and the faster turnover of skill obsolescence. A portfolio career can also appeal to younger cohorts of lawyers who want to travel, pursue their interests, and explore different work options, rather than following a traditional path to partnership. A portfolio career is overall a great choice for lawyers who do not fit in just one box and who value variety, continuous learning, and new challenges.

Examples of portfolio career lawyers include Amy Bird, employment lawyer at Clifford Chance and novelist; Alex Wade, a writer, libel lawyer, and journalist, having authored books and chapters on surfing, boxing, and football; Joanna Skurzewska, who combines consultant lawyer work with being a fine artist and photographer; and Mena Ruparel, an experienced family lawyer, who has built a portfolio career around her family law expertise, including consultancy, training, speaking, authorship, and arbitration. V, a corporate and commercial lawyer I spoke with, combines a 3-day part-time job as a consultant lawyer for two platform law firms with teaching, research, and writing. V states:

> *"I value the variety and broad horizons that having a portfolio career gives me. What appealed to me about being a consultant lawyer was freedom, a non-toxic environment, and being able to work when I want. Women lawyers who are mothers can create their own work–life blend and better earnings as a consultant lawyer, which is not always possible to achieve in private practice. My number one tip for women lawyers considering becoming a consultant lawyer is to do research on what makes you happy."*

Christina Blacklaws, former president of the Law Society and founder of Blacklaws Consulting, is also a portfolio careerist. Blacklaws has a strong specialism in legal tech, as well as diversity, equity, and inclusion (DEI), with components of her portfolio career including law firm retainers, non-executive roles, and keynote talks. Her advice to women lawyers considering consultancy is:

> *"Portfolio careerists like myself need to carve out time in a busy diary to take a step back and review. Looking at external trends and your own life stage go hand-in-hand. Career agility is a must in a fast-changing world of work and to maximize career fulfilment."*

However, while having a portfolio career offers the benefits of autonomy and flexibility, it can also be uncertain and unpredictable. Legal consultancy work, therefore, can be a great addition, as it enables lawyers to flex and develop other strings to their bow, such as paid talks and side gigs. Portfolio careers take active management to create, edit, and evolve. Getting expert from an experienced career strategist coach or personal marketing mentor can be very beneficial.

Conclusions

The number of women entering the legal profession has been slowly rising, but the percentage of women at the more senior ranks, especially in larger law firms with 50+ partners, is disproportionately low. Becoming a consultant lawyer is a fast-growing trend, as it presents an opportunity for women to side-step much of the bias embedded in the legal profession. Consultancy enables women lawyers to design a work–life balance that works for them; receive support in the form of compliance, governance, professional insurance, and the use of a modern and expedient tech platform; earn more for the effort they put in; be part of a supportive and collaborative community; avoid delegation bias; and take control of their careers. The growth of the consultant lawyer trend is set to continue, as it is likely that more young lawyers will choose this path. Gen Z desires more variety and greater responsibility in their careers than was possible for prior generations, such as Generation X, Baby Boomers, and Traditionalists.

To succeed, aspiring consultant lawyers must develop a career strategy and plan, build their legal specialism, network and grow their client following, and develop career capital and a compelling personal brand.

References

1 Codex Edge, *Platform Firms Report 2025*, 2025. See: https://www.codexedge.com/wp-content/uploads/2025/05/Platform-Firms-Report-2025.pdf

2 Setfords, "The Rise of Alternative Law Firms: Why Setfords is 'The Platform Firm to Watch'", 2022. See: https://consultantsolicitor.co.uk/the-rise-of-alternative-law-firms-why-setfords-is-the-platform-firm-to-watch/

3 Bright Horizons Family Solutions LLC, *MFI Legal Sector Cut 2025*, 2025. See: https://solutions.brighthorizons.co.uk/resources/research/mfi-legal-sector-cut-2025

4 *Ibid.*

5 *Ibid.*

6 Solicitors Regulation Authority, "Diversity in law firms' workforce", 3 January 2025. See: https://www.sra.org.uk/sra/equality-diversity/diversity-profession/diverse-legal-profession/

Chapter 12:
Your voice, your power: strategic amplification for women in law

By Joanne Brook, consultant lawyer, and Belinda Lester, managing director at Lionshead Law

Belinda and I worked together many years ago, forming an immediate friendship both in and outside of work. We both achieved partnership early in our careers: myself before children, and Belinda after her first child was born. It was at this point that, having initially set up her own consultancy rather than returning to full-time work in the City, Belinda was persuaded to join a partnership to head up its new employment department. Belinda immediately negotiated flexible working; however, but sitting in partners' meetings, she very soon realized that most law firms were undervaluing their female lawyers and applying criteria for progression that were wholly skewed against women.

Realizing that the "senior"/equity partners were all men whose home lives facilitated them working long hours in the office whilst all their household responsibilities were fulfilled by a domestic partner – and that the chances of them exiting the partnership in the next 10 years was small – Belinda began to devise a method of working and running a legal practice that could overcome these barriers and ensure that she did not have to choose between her professional or personal life. Belinda knew that this meant she must rethink the traditional law firm practice; so, she set up her own law firm in 2012. It was a virtual firm from the outset, with no set working hours, fixed fees, or retainers, and with an ethos of bringing your whole self to work. It would be her firm, her way, and on her terms; it would also be better for any women who had faced the same career conundrums with partnership progression as she had.

As a technology lawyer, I had enjoyed all the benefits of remote and flexible working since the millennium, having spent as much time working from home or clients' premises as in the office. An early practitioner in technology law, my gender had been an advantage, as it made me memorable – only a handful of women worked in tech law in the late 1990s, and they were all well-regarded, especially by each other. However, after 20 years in practice and three children (but only one period of maternity leave), I was growing tired of being the "token woman" in pitches for new clients and dispirited by the fact that, despite the work I brought in, after the financial crash of 2008, it seemed that the older partners were doubling down, determined to remain at the firm for as long as possible to maximize their pension. Of course, this was a good financial decision for them; however, it was bad for my career progression to equity and for those of the other salaried partners wanting to modernize the firm. At yet another partners' meeting held after office hours, which I knew would inevitably tip into an evening at the pub and a late meal, I watched time and trains slip away. I calculated how much the hourly rate in the room was, and what the overtime rate for the babysitter and the cost of a taxi would be as a percentage of my own hourly rate. I realized that I knew the names of all my male colleagues' kids, but most didn't even know I had children. Meeting the expectations of my fellow partners at a large West End firm, and dealing with equally tantrum-prone and demanding young children at home, meant I had lost my work–life balance. Everything was about juggling and compromise. When bemoaning this to Belinda, she invited me to join Lionshead Law.

All about you

Clearly, not everyone has the desire or opportunity to start their own firm as Belinda did, or to demand remote working "because that's what my clients do". However, drawing on Belinda's experience of setting up an all-female virtual law firm and my experience of building my practice within it, this chapter encourages you to amplify yourself and build a personal brand as a tool for business development and career progression. Whether you are a managing or training partner looking for ways to motivate and mentor; considering a career change, but not ready to let go of law; a returner to work; or someone who feels overlooked or undervalued, this chapter will examine what amplification means for you. You will learn how to "amp up" and why it is necessary as a means of building useful and useable business and referral networks for yourself and others; challenging prejudices; shattering glass ceilings; and forcing change.

Practice (verb): To carry out or perform a particular activity, method, or custom habitually or regularly

Bad habits, poor practice

Early on in her plans for a new-style firm, Belinda identified two big issues that stagnate progression in a professional practice . The first is structure: a senior partner gets work in and manages several salaried partners who, in turn, pass work to associates and then to junior lawyers and paralegals. The senior solicitor relies on the pyramid being retained to ensure their "margin" and, therefore, their partnership drawings. Bringing on new talent in their department means a division of the resources and potential for loss of income for the senior lawyer. This often leads to highly skilled lawyers waiting for a partner to retire or to leave the firm for their chance to progress to the senior departmental position.. The result can be disengagement from talented young lawyers who perceive their career to be stalling. Even worse, the most talented and ambitious might leave to join clients or competitors, or exit the profession out of sheer frustration at the inertia. In particular, Belinda had seen female friends in law suffer with "career inertia", often stagnating in their careers after maternity leave and perceiving colleagues to have "overtaken" them. These lawyers would chose to either move in-house or leave practice altogether for law-related work, where their qualification would be useful but not necessarily used to practice law.

The second issue is the apparent need for all the lawyers in the pyramidal structure of a firm to recover large amounts of time against a matter. This did not favor the efficient lawyers who would do the job in a shorter period of time to ensure standard office hours were kept and (importantly for many women lawyers) that childcare and other domestic responsibilities could also be achieved. As career progression in so many firms is based on billable hours or time recovered, anyone working efficiently and quickly – and, in particular, those lawyers (usually women) who were cramming five days' work into part-time working patterns – is clearly going to be disadvantaged by efficiencies designed to reduce time spent on matters.

Belinda saw that law firms of all sizes generally relied on the presence of an "unpaid partner" (assumed to be a wife or girlfriend) in the background, who ensured that domestic life and children were cared for while the "important work" was carried out in an office at all hours of the day and night, running up costs for the client (and driving down productive output from staff). She identified that much of the machismo culture of "jackets on seats" and "pulling an all-nighter" by completing deals at 2am is outmoded and unnecessary. The structures of many law firms facilitate this 24/7 and male-oriented culture, perpetuating biased working practices. These cannot be fixed without fundamental change.

From discussions with clients, Belinda also knew that the method of charging hourly fees seemed counter-intuitive for most; clients valued a quick turnaround, and on-point and relevant advice from someone who already knows the answer and can provide it at speed. In recognizing all of these factors, Belinda identified the opportunity to make a fundamental change to legal practice by getting rid of office hours and client-unfriendly hourly rates and rewarding consultants who choose when to work based on income generated.

A new firm and new way of working was formed, and Belinda knew that, by launching the firm, she could encourage other women who had been in the same position as her, who were coming to similar realizations about their career and who wanted to stay in law but enjoy fulfilling personal lives. That encouragement might spur them to join Lionshead Law, and seeing what she had done could empower them to believe it was possible to do things differently. Belinda knew that she could champion the idea and build a client base that bought into the new way of doing things. To build Lionshead Law and rebuild the Belinda brand, she had to "amplify" it all.

The old business development routine in many law firms was to model oneself on a senior lawyer in order to "step into their shoes", doggedly emulating the previous generations and their method of achieving success – be that through working long hours, sacrificing a social life, or immersing oneself in the law firm culture. Too often, networking in the legal profession favors historically male-oriented activities and spaces: rounds of golf; social events outside of office hours (often involving alcohol); residential conferences; and all-nighters to both complete work and to entertain and network with clients. Despite becoming more diverse, a startling number of law firms still operate in this way, designing their corporate activities and client entertainment around the needs of male clients and skipping over events with potentially greater appeal for women almost entirely.

Additionally, women lawyers – despite making up over half of qualified solicitors in the UK – still often find themselves either unable or unwilling to attend these events or activities, due to either personal commitments, a disinclination to socialize in a masculine environment, and anxieties about getting safely home late at night. They also face the internal battle between ambition and resentment, as they may have previously taken part in these events or activities only to realize that they were only brought along as a social nicety or to maintain appearances in regard to gender parity. Perhaps worse still is when women find themselves excluded due to previous "declined" invitations, compounded by a tendency to be apologetic about not fitting in with the plans of others, even when those are out of office and outside of working hours. It is particularly difficult for women in those legal fields dominated by men, who not only have to battle gendered expectations and prejudices, but who are then also supposed to think of new ways to market their work and services if it is not to be done as it has been in the past. Business development requires expanding client interactions beyond each matter and networking with others, but there is a need to recognize that, for women of all ages and backgrounds, doing this on a golf course or in a pub is generally unfavorable.

When she launched Lionshead, Belinda found that she needed to work out how to get clients in and – as a woman working from home with a young family – which primary methods she could use to differentiate and develop the business, without peddling the same brand of expertise and corporate entertainment as so many antediluvian male predecessors in traditional law firms.

Amplify (noun): To increase size or effect of something or add detail or information

What is amplification?

Amplification is using impactful statements in an environment where they can be expanded, passed on, and reused. It is seeing every engagement as a potential client matter or as having potential for a referral, and taking the chance to extend the reach of every engagement to a wider audience. It is mentoring; it is becoming a non-executive director and being willing to do all of this for others you respect. It might sound straightforward, but it takes time and commitment to identify the messages you want to present; to find the right medium that will broaden the impact and reach of your message; and follow up with those who engage with you, to build a network of mutual support, communications, referrals, and work.

What do we mean by AMPing up?

__A__im
__M__edia
__P__ersonality

Why amplify?

One of this book's aims is to provide a roadmap is to guide change; therefore, in the next part of this chapter, we offer some practical steps to take for women looking to "AMP up", because we believe (to misquote Socrates): "Let she who would move the world first move herself."

Taking Aim: choosing what to amplify

The first step in amplification is to ask yourself, "What is my Aim?" By this, we mean identifying what it is that you primarily want to achieve in practice and be known for. It is likely your needs will change over time so consider what is your primary focus at this point of your life and career? This focus might apply to current or past work or an intention to secure more work of that type.

For Belinda, when she started Lionshead Law, the "Aim" was to achieve flexibility and create direct and enduring working relationships with clients. Establishing her own business also meant that she could innovate as she wanted, and it made her the kind of business owner she was taking instructions from. This itself was an important marketing tool that could be "amplified" directly to clients in information about the firm, in discussions with other professionals, and across client and professional forums.

For me, the "Aim" was gaining diverse work within my field of interest. While this might sound contrary for a lawyer looking to specialize, I had realized early in my career that commercial contracts are fundamentally dull. Whichever way I looked at it, the best ones got put away in a drawer and forgotten, never needing to be consulted again – that felt a little unrewarding. So, my ambition was to engage with clients whose work and business output was interesting. Having taken aim at – and achieved – that work, I still gain energy and motivation from the innovative and ever-changing work undertaken by her clients in the creative sectors.

Continuing professional development (CPD) obligations require lawyers to "reflect on your knowledge and skills, and the quality of your practice", which is something you should also do to identify what it is that you want from your work in legal practice.[1] Some questions to ask yourself as you go undergo this process are:

1. What do I perceive that I do well?
2. What area of my practice makes me the most comfortable?
3. What part of my job gives me the most satisfaction?
4. What do others tell me I do well?
5. What matter-imperative or strategic workaround have I seen someone else use or adopt that I learnt most from?

6. What is the best example of an occasion that made me feel my voice and experience added value?

The first question might be simple to answer, but it might not be so straightforward to reflect on. It asks you to explore what you understand that you already do well – not what you could do well. Noting the answer to Question 4 should affirm your answer to Question 1. If others' perception of what you do well seems different to your own, think about whether it is a case of vocabulary or why the person you asked might characterize you in that way. This is important because law is all about communication, and progress in practice is driven by effective communication from you about your advice.

Answering Questions 2 and 3 will require some honest evaluation of your current role. When you are considering your answers, you might also try asking these questions in the negative, specifically to make you consider what you want to move away from, as knowing what you don't want to do is also key. Precisely because it is natural to enjoy what we are good at, and we will do it better at a task when we enjoy or are comfortable doing it – or at least believe that we do – we should find correlations between the answer for Question 1 and for Questions 2 and 3.

Questions 5 and 6 are intended to prompt you to think about how others do things well and about what achievements you have felt good about.

When you look back at your answers to Questions 1 and 6 – what you do well with what you feel good about in your job – they should align. If they don't, ask which elements the answers do share. Your desired Aim will be in those commonalities.

Mapping answers and Aims takes time and energy, and can be difficult to achieve within an hourly rate work structure. If that is the type of firm you work in, ask for your CPD and training targets; if you do not believe they are correct or do not provide sufficient time for you to practice amplification reflection, ask to extend them under time allocated for training and education or business development, so that this time is recognized and can be "spent" against targets. Your Aim becomes your personal manifesto for change and development, which can be useful in terms of measuring your progress.

The second step: choosing your Media

Most business development advisors will tell you to "get out there" and to "network hard", but the disadvantage of large networking events is that they have the breadth and quantity to appeal to as many people as possible, but not necessarily the capacity for depth. It is very hard to engage in any meaningful communications between mainstage speakers, in a "breakout room", before the after-dinner speech, or while balancing a drink, a canapé, and a delegate pack.

Smaller, local events can often act as support networks for start-ups and bootstrapped small businesses, whose owners have little or no need for legal services and whose only goal in being there might be to sell their own goods and services, rather than having a discussion with you. There remain barriers to attending networking events before and after usual office hours, especially if you have caring responsibilities or hesitancy about attending for any number of reasons.

When Belinda started Lionshead Law, it was going to be an entirely virtual practice (and it remains so), with no hourly rates and no normal working hours. It offered specialist legal law advice for fixed fees or on a monthly retainer at affordable rates, due to the minimal overheads. She chose the tagline "Always here for you..." to demonstrate to clients that advice was available even outside normal business hours, wherever and whenever they needed it. In choosing to use "Always here for you", Belinda acknowledged that the tagline was doing a lot of heavy lifting, but that meant it was apt for amplification. She could show new clients that this was a new firm, doing things differently; she could demonstrate to individuals that the approach they would receive would be one-to-one; it showed corporate clients that Lionshead intended to build a long-term working relationship with them, which also spoke to the retainer model. It could also be used in recruitment. With no "normal" hours, it meant the client no longer had an expectation that their advisor would be sitting at their desk between 9.00am and 6.00pm, Monday to Friday awaiting their call. Without that expectation, the solicitor advising could work entirely flexibly; they might be at a swim-meet, coming back from the school run, or out grabbing some shopping. Their lawyer could be at Costa Coffee or in Costa Rica – the client shouldn't care, so long as the advice given was good and it was given when they asked for it.

Sitting at her brand-new desk with her brand new-business, Belinda knew she had to focus her Aim, find the correct medium for communication, and generate work, so she asked herself what she was good at and when her voice and advice added value to a matter. Belinda determined that this happened most often in work with potential claimants, particularly those who could bring claims for uncapped damages and with less than two years' service whose dismissals are deemed "automatically unfair" or who have suffered unlawful discrimination. She asked, "Which group probably suffers most often from discrimination in the workplace?" Exactly the type of woman that Belinda was! Working mothers and women who have just had a baby.

With all of this to feed her ambition to build a brand and engage in business development, Belinda realized that the best possible advertising is doing a great job for someone and being referred by them to do work for someone else. As happy individuals are far more likely to refer work, and personal referrals at scale were likely to generate a bigger personal profile, leading to a bigger brand profile, this appeared the obvious way to secure work from more clients and secure the cycle of instructions and referrals. That is amplification.

Belinda's next questions were "where to go" to add value and "how to join those conversations she could add value to", thereby connecting with potential clients. Back in 2012, Belinda chose to commit her networking efforts to Facebook. Recognizing that (even if Facebook permitted it) direct selling rarely works in person and certainly does not work on Facebook, she joined groups where members wanted to talk to others in the same situation as they were. They often asked for advice; frequently, the guidance they sought was legal in nature, relating to their jobs, divorces, neighborhood disputes, conveyancing, or the establishment of their own businesses. In particular, Belinda found that the women in a group would either ask their question directly to the other members or, quite often, enquire if anyone in the group could recommend a solicitor. By becoming active in those groups, joining discussions and offering legal advice in response to a question, Belinda found (as you will, if you choose this as your medium) that, in a relatively short space of time, she became the solicitor that other members of the group recommended. You will also find that offering some free advice in a forum will frequently result in a direct message, which will then lead to a paid instruction. For Belinda, initially, Facebook felt like the right environment to reach out to groups where members discussed their problems and sought answers in the fields of employment, family, private client, and other "people-centered" areas of law. It allowed her to shape and build her profile, cement her authority, and get direct work, as well as gain introductions and referrals, which is at the very heart of amplification.

Despite working with technology, I have never used Facebook personally or as a forum for my work; my clients do not tend to look for help or advice there. When starting at Lionshead Law, I joined specialist networks where chief technology officers (CTOs) shared problems and discussed niche issues and new technology. Crucially, in these groups, I could discern where my clients spent their time on social media and why. Having Aimed at a variety of clients in creative sectors, I realized that what was important in building my practice was becoming a commentator on what was "new". By doing so, I would create a profile as a trusted advisor with interest in both current and future issues, demonstrating authority and thought leadership in specific fields. For me, LinkedIn was my "Media", supported by speaking at conferences and publishing articles to validate my voice and extend my profile.

In each instance, once you have identified your Aim and chosen your Media, you focus your efforts on your chosen field and those contiguous areas of work that outlie it, as it is likely that, in monitoring those, you will be able to identify the next big issue. You might decide that the work you want to Aim for is best suited to the medium of YouTube, Instagram, X, TikTok, Reddit, newspapers, technical press, conference papers, or academic publications – all are equally valid if they provide you with scope to AMP up. The foundation of amplification is picking the medium that will provide you with the most scope to expand your reach and grow your client base. That includes making contacts and engaging with other lawyers within the same sector, but in a complementary practice area. Follow those professionals that perform similar work to yours and engage with it. Engaging with others' work – and encouraging others to engage with yours – at least doubles your reach. Remember to ask clients to add comments to your posts (and thank them by name when they do) and to mention you in theirs, so that your coverage for referrals is always increasing.

It may be that you are returning to work after a career break and feel that you no longer have a professional network. However, you will have met hundreds of people in your personal life during your time away from a desk. Each one might be a client, all of them referrers, and the network that you have built up outside of the profession is as valid a base for amplification, gaining referrals, and acquiring experience as paid networking event or organization. Experience outside of the office gives you practical insight and experience, and you should not be shy in applying these. By bringing your whole self to your work, you exclude nobody else.

The human touch: adding your Personality

Law and legal service provision is primarily a communication business; to build trust, clients need to feel that they can express themselves to and connect with their advisor. When developing your own brand, so that you and others can amplify it, blandness is not an option. You need to be professional and personable, which means showing some personality; nothing adds to a post, article, talk (or chapter!) like a bit of character. Whether that is as an extrovert litigator who unapologetically fights a case with utter conviction and crows about the brilliance of their argument, or as a thoughtful commercial lawyer who is steadfast in a negotiation and whose calm rhetoric seeks settlement and collaboration, the personal touch and personality of the professional engaged by a client is key to the experience of the client when it comes to legal engagement. While expertise is imperative, Personality is crucial in amplification, differentiating you from your competition and humanizing the content you prepare, rendering legal service provision more accessible to both current and potential clients.

AI and you: artificial intelligence's role in amplification

Discussing the critical nature of trust and the human touch in legal engagement is a good place to consider the elephant in the room; the big grey thing in the corner of your vision that you think you know. However, in real life, it's a lot bigger and more powerful than you anticipated, isn't it? Yes, we are speaking of artificial intelligence (AI). Another chapter deals directly with AI, but let us examine it briefly here because, in some ways, its rise validates the need for amplification.

Since 2012, I have worked with clients who create Big Data and developing large language models (LLMs) to feed AI programs; as such, I have heard the questions they ask of it, seen the joy of programmers when their product "earns", and witnessed the bafflement of CTOs when it provides an unexpected response that is brilliant or – just as often – bogus and biased. I approach AI with a degree of healthy skepticism – based not on being disinclined to use it, but on watching and learning about how it has been created as an all-powerful tool that can be put to all manner of uses we have yet to identify. I know that "with great power comes great responsibility" (quoting Spiderman or Napolean, depending on your own biases), but invention and innovation historically has generally been achieved irresponsibly (with exceptions). I view AI as one of the least responsible innovations ever devised, knowingly using biased data for training, which is conducted without true rigor and with minimal oversight by people playing with money for a prize that will always be disputed.[2]

We are certain that the rise in the use of human-like technology in legal practice will mean that the human touch, connection, and personality will become ever more important in professional service provision. AI strikes at the heart of what lawyers do: skilled work requiring accumulated knowledge and experience, applied with the ability to reliably predict an outcome and strategize about it. It is inevitable that clients will demand greater use of this technology by law firms if the outcome can be more assured, because the knowledge set used to determine it is so much more vast, and if it can be done faster, more accurately, and at lower cost to the client. Additionally, the use of AI in case management and practice will fundamentally change how teams are managed, and by whom. The Lawyers on Demand 2025 Global Survey Report *The Great Reinvention* concluded that legal teams are "dealing with a seemingly impossible contradiction", in which the processes and structures supposed to help them manage caseloads are often adding to the pressure via data inundation and system obligations.[3] Practitioners are all too conscious of the demands of those dual despots: compliance and case management. Herein lies the paradox: gaining access to AI that can assist lawyers to perform their job more comprehensively can lead to those same lawyers losing their jobs to AI because of cost, efficiency, and client expectations. In this landscape, it becomes even more important to be seen and heard as a practitioner.

We know that AI poses a threat to how law is practiced and to jobs within the legal profession. We know that there are currently issues with reliability in legal AI: false biographies and fake case law (hallucinations) range from 64 to 88 percent[4] in response to specific legal queries put to the AI. However, we need to remember that human lawyers also make mistakes. The UK's Solicitors Regulation Authority identified this as a known (but not new) factor in its November 2023 Risk Outlook Report and cautioned that "errors by an AI system could affect many more people than errors by a single person could".[5] This informs us that, even if AI can work "better", there are some specialist areas of law where humans still want to connect with humans for advice. As a professional in a role that is being comprehensively disrupted and will be overhauled, it is more important than ever to find your own voice and personality and establish connections with clients, both directly and via third parties, to become a trusted advisor that is called upon in times of crisis to focus on a single aspect of their life or business, while AI fulfils all other legal needs for them.

AI is clearly a threat to jobs within the legal profession – in fact, to the legal profession as a whole – but it is also an incredibly useful tool in summarizing cases, crunching data, reading contracts, providing case law, writing letters of advice, and finding precedent. It can also be an incredibly useful tool to generate a profile for you and to help you to brand yourself and your communications. Through use of an AI tool (e.g., ChatGPT and others), you can create your mission statement and a portfolio of messages; plan a schedule for those messages; and have a PR consultancy in your pocket to guide you. However, a word of caution here – so can everyone else, so use it judiciously.

Amp (verb): To increase the level or amount of (something) sharply; to make (someone) feel excited and full of energy

AMP yourself

You have your Aim, Media, and Personality locked down; now you need to actually comment, post, and opine online. Create content that is evergreen (AI is useful here) that can be used repeatedly, perhaps with a different introduction or a refocus while maintaining the core message. Evergreen content that has been read, re-read, reposted, and quoted multiple times over an extended period reinforces your position as a voice of authority. Content that is understandable and broken down into a format that highlights issues and provides answers is more likely to be commented on and reposted. It is also the most adaptable content, as it can be reused in different ways, including by others.

Adding your voice to ongoing conversations is another way to amplify, as the discourse grows and the reach spreads. Draw on your own experiences (both positive and negative) to make connections. Both Belinda and I have found ourselves the only women in the room. I have found myself being expected to make tea in the meeting (why else was I there?) because of my youth and gender; now, many years on, being of "a certain age", I am often overlooked, as we are indoctrinated towards youth and maleness as the image of authority. I've power-dressed and I've pouted; I have even left the room when voices became raised, telling everyone I would return when they had calmed down (in another life, I may have been a headteacher!). However, I now recognize that my amplification comes from my knowledge – both in and out of the office – and that being the unexpected one to lead can be a real strength.

Amplification also means finding the people who will complement the work you do and inviting them into the conversation. For both Belinda and I, this has changed over time. New groups with different interests join and disband and people come and go, but being given a voice to express your ideas remains. Social media has expanded your reach exponentially. You can add specific topics of interest to the evergreen content you produce; the more accessible and understandable your content is, and the more relevant it is to specific issues, the more likely it is to be quoted and reposted and thus amplified by others with a voice and audience who want to promote relevant content and fill their feeds with interesting, useful information. However, it is a fact that social media is a voracious consumption machine of content and attention, so you should be disciplined about posting content and engaging with it and others regularly. Again, AI can be your assistant if you find yourself short on time or need some practical tips on this.

By joining conversations, we can influence and inform; by creating a platform for yourself, you can be heard; and by giving advice, you will find solutions. This is amplification, which brings change.

Final words

Neither Belinda nor I were in the 7 percent of British people who are educated privately.[6] Additionally, neither of us started higher education wanting to be solicitors: Belinda's first degree is in psychology, and mine is in business law. However, we have both extended our academic and professional qualifications beyond our first degrees and have remained in law and in partnership, despite personal challenges, raising children, and various caregiving responsibilities. Neither of us would do any of it differently.

References

1 Solicitors Regulation Authority, "Understanding your continuing competence requirements", 2 April 2025. See: https://www.sra.org.uk/solicitors/resources/continuing-competence/understanding-continuing-competence/

2 Open Computing Facility, "The Loebner Prize", 2025. See: https://www.ocf.berkeley.edu/~arihuang/academic/research/loebner.html

3 Lawyers on Demand, *The Great Reinvention: Reclaiming control of legal work*, 2024. See: https://cdn.prod.website-files.com/6706d0c620be3bd3a6954c8e/67ee48f342e9e33b39690f8e_BM.SP0108.B percent20- percent20LOD percent20Global percent20Survey percent20Report_2024 percent205.pdf

4 Dahl M, Magesh V, Suzgun M, and Ho D.E., "Hallucinating Law: Legal Mistakes with Large Language Models are Pervasive", Stanford Human-Centered Artificial Intelligence, 11 January 2024. See: https://law.stanford.edu/2024/01/11/hallucinating-law-legal-mistakes-with-large-language-models-are-pervasive/

5 Solicitors Regulation Authority, "Risk Outlook report: The use of artificial intelligence in the legal market", 20 November 2023. See: https://www.sra.org.uk/sra/research-publications/artificial-intelligence-legal-market/

6 Social Mobility Commission, "Press release: Elitism in Britain, 2019", 24 June 2019. See: https://www.gov.uk/government/news/elitism-in-britain-2019

About Globe Law and Business

Globe Law and Business was established in 2005. From the very beginning, we set out to create legal books that are sufficiently high level to be of real use to the experienced professional, yet still accessible and easy to navigate. Most of our authors are drawn from Magic Circle and other top commercial firms, both in the United Kingdom and internationally. Our titles are carefully produced, with the utmost attention paid to editorial, design and production processes. We hope this results in high-quality publications that are easy to read and a pleasure to own.

In 2021, we were very pleased to announce the start of a new chapter for Globe Law and Business following the acquisition of law books under the imprint Ark Publishing. Our law firm management list is now significantly expanded with many well-known and loved Ark Publishing titles.

We are also pleased to announce the launch of our online content platform, Globe Law Online, which allows for easy access across firms. Details of all titles included can be found at www.globelawonline.com. Email glo@globelawandbusiness.com for further details and to arrange a free trial for you or your firm.

We'd very much like to hear from you with your thoughts and ideas for improving what we offer. Please do feel free to email me on sian@globelawandbusiness.com. Happy reading and thank you for your time.

Sian O'Neill
Managing director
Globe Law and Business
www.globelawandbusiness.com

www.ingramcontent.com/pod-product-compliance
Ingram Content Group UK Ltd.
Pitfield, Milton Keynes, MK11 3LW, UK
UKHW052228130126
466916UK00003B/28

9 781837 231379